British Toy Trains

Featuring all those other British toy train manufacturers

Book 1 of 4 - Whitanco, Burnett, Chad Valley, Palitoy, Astra, DCMT

This is Book 1 of what is hoped will be a series of four books outlining the full history of these wonderful toys.

Book 2 will cover Betal, Mettoy Co. Ltd., and A. Wells Co. Ltd. Hopefully to be published in September, 2015.

Book 3 will cover the huge range of Brimtoy Ltd., Hopefully to be published early 2016.

Book 4 will cover Bowman, Bar Knight, Marx and various small companies.

We also plan, by prior order only, a hard bound set of all four books in a special case, on completion of the series.

First published in the United Kingdom
2015 by Michael D. Foster.

© Michael D. Foster.

All rights reserved. No part of this book may be reproduced or utilized in any form or by any means, whether electronic or mechanical, including photocopying or recording, or by any information storage and retrieval system without permission in writing from the copyright holder.

Design & Photography: Michael Bowes.

Printed in Spain under the supervision of MRM Graphics Ltd, Winslow, Bucks, MK18 3DZ

ISBN 978-0-9932047-0-8

In Appreciation

This book only appears thanks to the skill, experience and enthusiasm of Michael Bowes. I have spent thirty years researching these manufacturers, finding the models and material, but it is Michael who has put it all together so I am extremely grateful to him.

So many people have helped me with information, models, pieces of the jigsaw that I feel I must thank them all. Going through my correspondence files is easy – and sad. Many are no longer with us, but, as the Remembrance Day Service records, - "We will remember them".

Michael D. Foster. 11th November 2014

Viv Alexander	Jeff Carpenter	Colin Duthie	Simon Hailey	Ian Layne	Henry Pearce	James Skoyles
Arthur Ashard	Len Champion	David Embling	Philip Hamilton	Ian Leonard	Bryan Pentland	Cecil Slator
Colin Atkins	Albert Chaplin	Richard Elkan	John Hardy	Bruce Macdonald	Barry Potter	David Smith
Colin Atkinson	Tom Clark	Adrian Feather	Doug Harris	Peter McAskie	David Pressland	Peter Smith
Albyn Austin	Barrie Clarke	John Forman	Lester Harrison	Tony Manthos	John Procter	Joe Swain
Charles Baeker	John Clibbon	Harry Foster	Chris Hawling	John Marr	Steve Pryer	Jim Taylor
Mark Bailey	Rev. Alan Cliff	Jack Gahan	Mike Hobday	George Marshall	David Ramsey	Jack Tempest
Myke Barritt	Mike Cooke	Bill Garnett	Peter Hilton	John Mayo	David Ranson	Mike Tomkins
Graham Bilbe	Peter Corley	Rex George	Russell Horne	Nathan Middeldorf	John Ridley	John Van Riemsdijk
Harry Billington	Ken Cowls	Phil Goater	Ron Ingram	John Neale	Julian Ryder	Ned Williams
Derek Brough	John Cross	David Gordon	Brian Kelly	Nicholas Oddy	Lester Saunders	Paul Williams
Mike Brown	Michael Dawe	Simon Goodyear	Mike King	Don Palmer	Frank Sharman	Carl Whiteley
Roger Brown	Mike Delaney	Chris Graebe	Dave Lambourne	Ian Paterson	Peter Shelley	Jim Whittacker
Joyce Buttigieg	Nat Donnelly	Dean Green	Eric Large	Stan Peachey	Ken Simmons	Peter Wolveridge

SOMETIMES I THINK WE ARE ALL NUTS

I dedicate this book to my grandchildren, Charlie (8) and Ollie (6) Pickens. The new generation!

This is the first, to my knowledge, in depth study of all those wonderful toy trains produced in their thousands and sold for the most part, cheaply in such famous stores as Woolworths and the like. From 1919 to 1959, some forty years, these colourful tinplate toy trains fired the imagination of young boys who could only dream. Certainly, the models of Bassett Lowke, Hornby and Leeds were out of reach of the younger clients, being purchased by their parents or the more mature enthusiast. Yet, these toys and at times exaggerated boxes had such appeal, despite their relatively low performance. Three or four circuits of the track, and you were done and had to rewind.

However, the more substantial models, in thicker tinplate, produced by Whitanco, Mettoy and Chad Valley had very professional clockwork mechanisms. By 1952, both Mettoy and Chad Valley had U2 powered battery locomotives. Mettoy even produced 3-rail tinplate track and electric, 4.5 volt models from 1937 to 1940.

I have endeavoured to set out, company by company, each model they produced, showing each locomotive, carriage, wagon and accessory with the date of manufacture. This will enable you to identify whatever model you have or had. The range is staggering. Little wonder it has taken me thirty years research. I hope you enjoy the result. I dedicate this book to the directors, engineers and workers who designed and manufactured these wonderful toys for us all.

Michael D. Foster
1st August 2013

CONTENTS

Introduction	6
Preface	7
The Rise of the British Tin Toy Industry	10
Whitanco	13
The Burnett Co. Ltd.	39
The Chad Valley Trains	51
The Palitoy Train Sets	115
Astra	126
DCMT Ltd	128

Introduction

At last! An innovative and complete book about early 'Made in Britain' toy trains. Compiled and studied by Michael Foster over many years, this work fills a gap that has been vacant far too long. Unfortunately delays due to illness, advising on exploration drilling and other matters took their toll. But the hold up has been worth the wait.

Mike is best known for his complete meticulous treatise on Hornby Dublo trains. That book, in the New Cavendish series, is known as the 'Hornby Dublo Bible' to admirers of this 00 gauge line. Now Mike has concentrated on the inexpensive, but colourful tinplate trains of yesteryear which in many cases, lasted into the late 60's.

During World War 1, Britain restricted imports from Germany to the United Kingdom and Government encouraged British toy manufacturers to produce toy trains. This book will tell you the whole story and make you aware of what came first. Delightfully naive, they are charming reminder of the past and great Collectors' items. The author, Michael Foster and many others, myself included, adore these trains. Mike has assembled a complete collection of these delights, and they appear in this book. It is appropriate to mention the late Ian Layne, whom also loved these toys.

This work is not only suitable for the train collector, but for those making a collection of all tinplate toys.

Nathan Middeldorf

Preface

Toy trains, or 'The Perfect Table Railway', so promoted by Meccano Ltd., in the launch of their Hornby-Dublo system, are older than you think. This wonderful satirical cartoon appeared in the magazine 'Fun' on the 2nd November, 1872. Some nineteen years later, the famous Marklin company set the gauge standard at the Leipzig Spring Fair. It pleads that the Directors of Railway Companies should at least gain some experience in controlling a railway before being let loose on the real thing, with the unfortunate carnage that followed. Marklin sold many of their cheaper sets through Gamages, the famous London store in Holborn while Gebruder Bing through Bassett Lowke.

In 1906, 152 different British outline model engines were on offer from six German manufacturers. Little wonder almost half of the entire toy train production was being exported to Britain. By 1910, every town in the country had a toy shop, departmental store or cycle shop selling Nuremberg toy trains. By 1914, when the book 'Off by Train' was published by Blackie and Son Ltd., this colour drawing of a Gauge 1 clockwork train was typical of layouts up and down the country. The market was saturated and the German companies were leap frogging each other in technical or quality advances. The First World War, the Great War, brought an immediate halt to this trade. The Department of Trade and Industry in London immediately set up meetings to induce British entrepreneurs and factories to take over this market. Obviously such companies were consumed by war work, so it was not until 1919 that the birth of the British toy train industry began. Once the horror of the war was ended, the Nuremberg factories once more flooded the British market with old stock and low prices. Only the more robust companies like Meccano, who introduced their Hornby Trains in 1920, and Brimtoy Ltd., and Wells Ltd., were able to survive and grow.

FUN.—NOVEMBER 2, 1872.

A SUGGESTION.

A NEW GAME, IN HUMBLE IMITATION OF KRIEGSPIEL, TO ENABLE RAILWAY DIRECTORS TO CONDUCT THEIR EXPERIMENTS WITHOUT LOSS OF LIFE; AND TO TEACH THEM THEIR BUSINESS GENERALLY.

"THE TRAIN TRAVELLED DOZENS OF MILES THAT AFTERNOON"

A famous and virtually unknown company, Whitanco Ltd., (Whiteley, Tansley Ltd., of Liverpool) were crippled by the market conditions. Though started in 1912, they commenced their toy train production in 1919. They called in the Receiver in 1921 and closed fully their toy production in 1924. They did however, move into the new wonder of the age – Radio, but more of them later.

How toy trains featured in 1898.

By happy chance, I knew them. They are the elder brother and sister of my to be Mother-in-Law, Diana. Adrian Hainsselin (1896-1977) and Dorothy Hainsselin (1894-1985)

BRITISH MADE CLOCK= WORK MECHANICAL TOYS

Royal Mail. Retail Price, 1/-

British Made.
By British Labour.
With British Material.

Two Models for this Season's Trade.

Delivery commencing October.

Samples ready for Inspection now.

INQUIRIES from wholesale merchants and shippers will be forwarded if addressed c/o Box No. 97, *Games and Toys*, Sicilian House, Sicilian Avenue, London, W.C. Retail dealers will be put in communication with the nearest wholesale houses if inquiries are addressed as above. In view of the amount of correspondence entailed, and of the fact that up to the present there has been insufficient time to communicate with all wholesale houses, we ask prospective clients' indulgence for any slight delay there may be in communicating addresses of wholesale merchants. Every inquiry will be answered as quickly as possible.

Motor Bus Company. Retail Price, 1/-

POINTS IN WHICH WE SURPASS FOREIGN MADE GOODS.

- A heavier and more substantial gauge of material is used in the construction.
- Better, stronger and more substantial clockwork is supplied.
- More attention is paid to the printing—the colour and figures being excellent reproductions.
- All wheels, axles, springs and moving parts are made extra strong.
- Article for article, the size is as large and the appearance better.

Please mention "Games & Toys" when writing to advertisers.

---

468. TONGS.   470. WORKSHOP.   471. LARGE SHEARS.

Tinsmiths' tools as used in the nineteenth century and very much later.

Taken from Metal Box, a history by W. J. Reader.
Published by Heinemann, London. 1976.

YOU MAKE THE TOYS
WE MAKE THE MECHANISMS

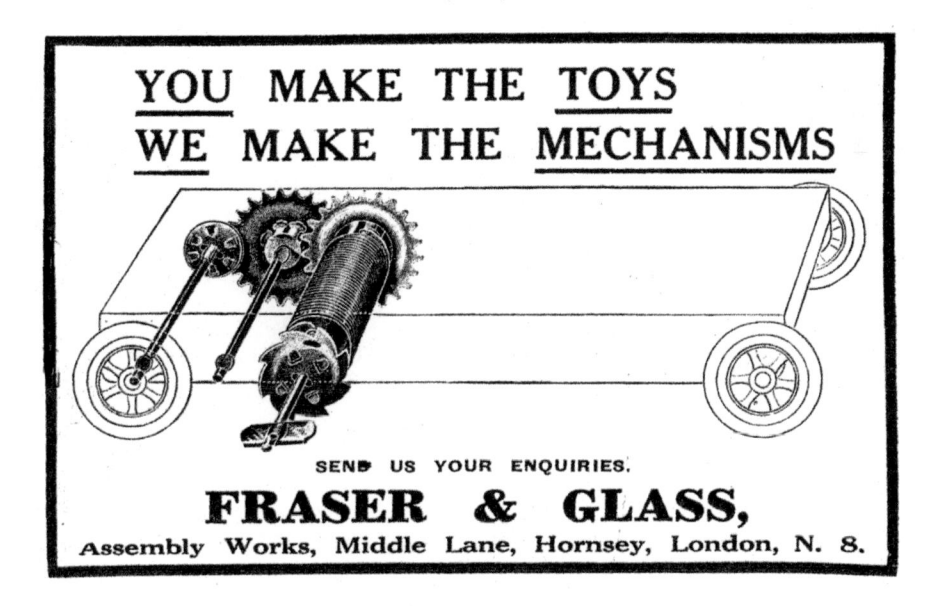

SEND US YOUR ENQUIRIES.

FRASER & GLASS,

Assembly Works, Middle Lane, Hornsey, London, N. 8.

The Rise of the British Tin Toy Industry

"An important trade," says the 1895 edition of Mrs Beeton's Book of Household management, "has sprung up within the last quarter of the century in tinned foods of various kinds."

I seemed to recall learning from my schooldays it commenced around the period of the Crimea War. It was the start of convenience foods, preserved foods out of season and was initially for the food and tobacco trade. Large scale can making did not begin to really develop in Britain until the 1930s. The firm Williamsons of Worcester produced 23 million cans in 1928, in 1930 some 115 million and by 1937, 335 million. Just under half were for milk and cream. The rest was for fruit and vegetables – the notorious 'processed peas'.

There were numerous small can makers around the country long before this. Edward C. Barlow and Sons, Ltd., had been making tin boxes from 1869. Hudson Scott Ltd., of Carlisle set up a factory in Workington where they produced luggage trucks, sentry boxes and other "Nursery Delights". What a marvellous description. These companies – with others such as Barringer, Wallis and Manners Ltd., of Mansfield, were making by the mid 1890s, fancy tins for biscuits, toffees, tobacco, cigarettes, sweets, mustard etc. This was the start of branded, easily recognisable goods for the mass market and found ready buyers

The ingenuity of the manufacturers produced superb works of art in the shape of colourful vases, books, golf bags, motor cars, Anne Hathaway's cottage, birds, beasts and toys. The appeal and use of the box long after it's contents had been used up being a major factor in it's original purchase.

Now we must understand these companies – brought so brilliantly together in the 1920s to form the Metal Box Company, were out and out 'Tin Bashers'. The exquisite designs so collectable today relied on visual appeal for a successful sale and helped balance the humdrum mass production items. These companies were not, and made no claim to be – 'mechanical engineers', so such things as good clockwork motors were beyond them. These were made by such companies as Fraser and Glass Ltd.

Up to the start of the First World War in 1914, the famous Nuremberg toy companies supplied magnificent steam, clockwork and electric powered toys. Bing alone employed over 4,000 workers and these wonderful companies had the complete monopoly of the toy trade.

The British Board of Trade hastily convened meetings to energise British companies to fill the gap which lead to such companies as Whitanco Ltd., Brimtoy - (British Metal and Toy Manufacturers Ltd.) and Barringer, Wallis and Manners Ltd., commencing toy production. A. Wells and company was formed in 1919 and even the famous Meccano company did not start making their to be world famous trains until 1920.

I put the failure of the toys produced by the 'Tin Bashers' to be on their weak clockwork mechanisms and the subsequent low play value they gave their owners. Now it is part of their appeal – times change. The tin companies could print and stamp and assemble superb toys, but had immense problems with the small mechanisms needed.

I had thought that surplus tools came from the Nuremberg toy companies and were sold to companies like Wells, Brimtoy and Whitanco and others. Now I am not so sure. There are strange, uniform designs in British livery that appear and it creates a nightmare for identification by enthusiasts such as you and I. Copies, possibly, but thanks to magnificent research by that doyen of toy train historians, Nicholas Oddy, we learn that Whitanco started as a tool makers.

They actually supplied the German Toy industry with tooling. So, with that market totally closed by the war, they sold tools to British companies and started to actually produce their own toys, once their war work was over.

The cost of such toys is always in the tooling. One must ensure a sufficient quantity of production is made to meet a critical price to ensure successful sales. That is why the same tooling/stamping models appear time after time under a variety of colours and lithography.

That is why also models become dated in appearance. The companies could not afford the new tools for modern outline models. Perhaps they could not be certain of selling sufficient models to recover their costs. By the mid 1950's, it was a falling market for mass produced '0' gauge trains. Tin toys needed mass production to be successfully priced for the public, just like other tin products. I read in Mr. W.J.Reader's superb history of Metal Box Ltd. (published by William Heinemann Ltd., in 1976) of a distraught Sales Director complaining that – "prices were cut until we were haggling about one eighth of a penny, per gross (144) on things like boot polish tins."

The law of the market place – the supply and demand – I find a fascinating study. Nothing changes!

THE MODEL RAILWAY c. 1950

This lovely picture, so nostalgic to me, is taken from 'The Wonder Book of Things to Do', published by Ward, Lock and Co. Ltd in 1950. It typifies my layout in an upper attic bedroom - my Train Room - in the The Manor, Sutton Coldfield, my home from 1948 to 1966.

I had an almost identical layout with Chad Valley trains. I had their sturdy, superb track, wooden stations and bridges, Britains Ltd., trees, hedges and farmyard animals. I would spend hours here, lost in an imaginary world, though never owning an engine like this. Mine was a truly toy train layout with crepe paper as grass or meadow, corrugated paper as a ploughed field, etc. My little 0-4-0 engine ran for hours. Pride of the line was the large blue, clockwork Chad Valley De Luxe 4-4-0 engine and tender, with their lovely 'tube' bogie coaches.

Little did I think, sixty years later, I would be collecting such. I still have all my old Britains farmyard animals and accessories. Happy days indeed.

So here, company by company, I present their story and their products.

Whitanco

Whitanco

'Whitanco?'
'Yes, Whitanco,' I replied.
'Never heard of them.' He replied – and neither had I in twenty five years of collecting toy trains. In 1985 I was visiting a, to me, new evening toy fair in Blackheath, North West Birmingham on the Wolverhampton road. I had had my Hornby Dublo book published just a few years earlier and was contentedly browsing the tables. I spotted this '0' gauge GNR open wagon, clearly marked 'Whitanco'. I had never heard of this make before and was intrigued. It was obviously of 'commercial' manufacture. What, I dreamed, if there were carriages, a locomotive even? I asked around, only to be met by a blank stare. It was new to everyone.

It was Simon Goodyear, bless him, that wonderful man, a long time friend and supplier of old toy trains, who unlocked it for me by sending me a photocopy of an advertisement he had found in the Boy's Own Paper for December, 1921. The Whitanco trains were manufactured by the Whiteley, Tansley Co. Ltd., of Beech Street, Liverpool 13.

THE "WHITANCO"
Superb Clockwork Train Set.
A REAL RAILROAD, PERFECT IN EVERY DETAIL,
FOR **50/-** COMPLETE.
BEAUTIFULLY BOXED.

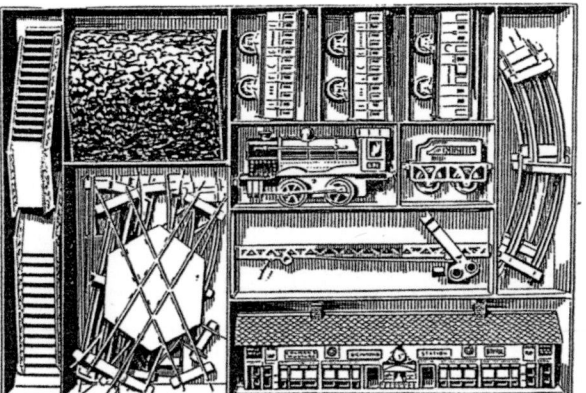

COMPRISING:
STRONG LONG RUNNING ENGINE,
TENDER,
TWO CARRIAGES,
GUARD'S VAN,
STATION,
TUNNEL,
BRIDGE & SIGNALS,
UPRIGHT SIGNAL,
REAL DETACHABLE LAMP,
RIGHT AND LEFT HAND SWITCH POINT,
CROSSING,
AND
ELEVEN CURVED AND FOUR STRAIGHT LINES MAKING 240 INCHES OF RUNNING RAILWAY TRACK—LENGTH OF TRAIN 30 INCHES.

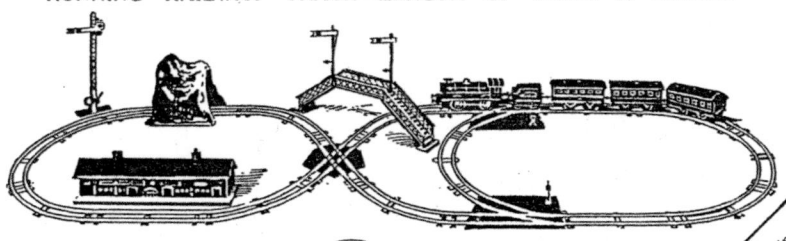

INSIST ON SEEING THIS TRADE MARK.
TRADE MARK.

Manufactured Entirely at the Whitanco Works by
WHITELEY, TANSLEY & Co., Ltd.,
(Dept. B.O.P.) BEECH ST., LIVERPOOL.

Should you experience any difficulty in obtaining this railway outfit from your dealer's send us a post card for particulars with your full name and address.

B.O.P. 19.] *When Buying anything Advertised in these pages please say that you saw the advertisement in the B.O.P.*

Simon Goodyear, that wonderful man, with Lou under the watchful eyes of Spencer. (Photograph: Paul Lumsdon)

A three hour search in the Public Records Office, Kew, brought to light a skeleton of the company background. They were registered on the 12th April, 1912. Mr. Ernest Whiteley was managing director and his brother, James William Whiteley, works manager. The other two directors were Mr. Arthur James Tansley and Mr. Frank Wedgewood. The Rev. Alan Cliff, another dear friend and author of 'Jack, the Station Cat' series records in his researches that Mr. Whiteley was a toolmaker and Mr. Tansley a turner. Mr. Whiteley is thought to have worked for Meccano Ltd., at one time, while Mr. Tansley had worked for the Auto Telephone Company.

Their homes were close together, Mr. Ernest Whiteley living at 120 Northwood Street, moving in 1913 to 68, Claremont Road. Mr. James Whiteley was at 'Lynwood', Broad Green and Mr. Arthur Tansley was at 69, Ennismore Road, Old Swan before moving to 37, Church Road, Stanley. Mr. Frank Wedgewood was just down the road at 16, Ennismore Road, Old Swan.

On the 28th August, 1913, they were joined by Mr. William Constantine of 62, Southdale Road. He had worked for Messrs. Robinsons, who manufactured geysers and gas fires. I don't know their original location, but on the 30th May, 1916, the company moved to 'The Lindens" formerly Beech Mount. This was a large house with, to quote the records –'a coach house, stables, a conservatory, factory, workshop etc.', in Beech Street, Liverpool. Their attractive trademark was first registered on the 24th January, 1916.

They were predominately toolmakers, supplying tools to many European toy manufacturers. Indeed, a large part of their business before the First World War was to the German toy industry. I do not think they started making toys themselves until 1915. Only twenty five percent of their production being so employed, the rest being on war work.

Whitanco had their first full page advertisement in the December issue of Games and Toys, the leading trade magazine, in 1916. (page 282). The following April issue, 1917 (page 559) had an advertisement by S. Erhard and Co. of 8, Bradford Avenue, London EC1, featuring their toys. It showed a carpet loco and a horse drawn cart.

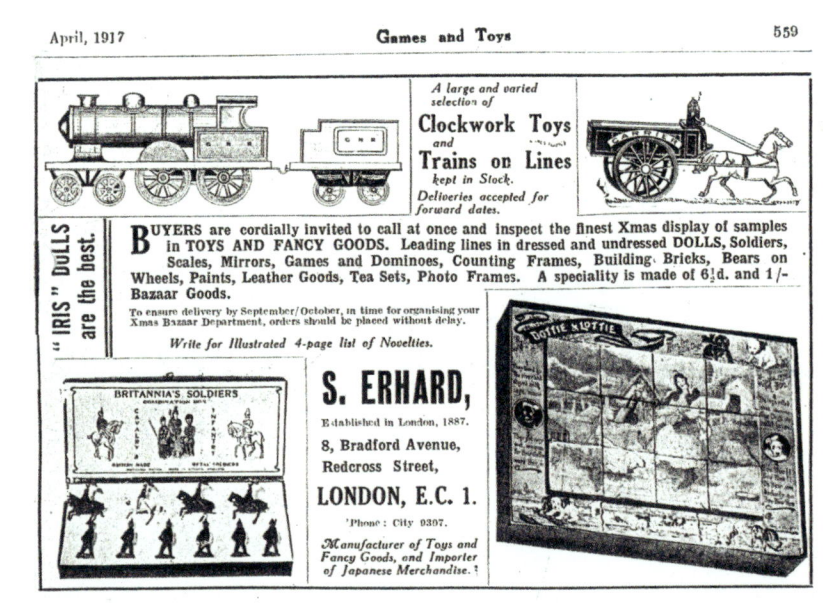

Their carpet engine was a GNR loco and tender, though thanks to Mr. David Pressland, he found for me a delightful CR (Caledonian Railway) version, still needing a tender!

There are some fascinating pictures of a Whitanco American carpet train and a set running on rails, complete with a cowcatcher! I am sure they exist. I would love to find one.

American Train Set

C 7. American Engine, Tender and 2 Coaches, 26 inches long.

American Passenger Train on Lines

F 8. American Engine, Tender, 2 Coaches and Guard's Van, 10 Lines. 31½ inches long.

American Goods Train on Lines

F 9. American Engine, Tender, 2 Trucks, 8 Lines. 25½ inches long

G. N. R. Engine and Tender.

C3. **G.N.R. Engine and Tender,** Mechanical, 12½ inches long, original colours.

Mr. Nicholas Oddy found the transcript in the Public Records office in Kew (File BT 55/80) of the meetings between the Board of Trade and the major toy manufacturers in 1922, including Mr. Frank Hornby of Meccano Ltd., and Mr. Ernest Whiteley. The Board of Trade had urged British manufacturers in 1914 to start making toys to compete with the virtual monopoly of the German Nuremberg manufacturers. The British companies thought they would be protected by import tariffs or the like, but this was not to be. The Nuremberg manufacturers once more commenced their production in November, 1919. Helped by the collapse of the German economy and fall in the value of the Deutsche Mark, the British companies simply could not compete.

They tried, however. They really tried. Innovative, entrepreneurial, one of the most impressive Whitanco models was a First World War Tank. It was a brilliant piece of machinery and now very rare. W. Butchers and Sons of Primus Engineering fame introduced their model tank in the December, 1916, issue of Games and Toys, just three months after the very first tank action on September 15th. Then, a single tank, leading two companies of infantry, succeeded in clearing a mile of enemy trenches, taking 370 prisoners for the loss of just five men. The Royal Tank Corps itself was not formed until July 28th, 1917.

December, 1916   Games and Toys   305

The Tank Arrives in Toyland.

It is no exaggeration to say that the arrival of Messrs. W. Butcher & Sons' "Primus" Tank has created a sensation in the toy trade. Within a day or two of the first authoritative pictures of the Tank being published in English papers, Messrs. Butcher astonished the big London dealers by ding them round a wonderful model constructed from the parts in one of the "Primus" sets. We need not comment on its faithful reproduction to the real thing, our illustration making this sufficiently obvious. Buyers instantly recognised that had here a topical line of extraordinary interest, and they hastened to give it great prominence in their windows, where it speedily attracted a crowd. The first one sent to a noted West End stores was purchased for £10, although its actual cost to construct was probably 30s. Another house iediately ordered a reproduction of a battlefield with trenches, shell holes and entanglements, to be built in their window, and at the present moment we believe it is finished, and a "Primus" Tank can be seen negotiating all obstacles. At Gamage's, again, the Press have sent up representatives to ask permission to photograph it, and a scene was quickly arranged in which a Tank was depicted demolishing a "Dometo" sugar refinery. Scarcely anyone believes that this model can be easily constructed from "Primus" engineering parts, yet there is nothing additional in it at all except the driving bands carrying the caterpillar feet which are simply made of webbing. The model takes but little time to construct, and there is nothing difficult in doing so whatsoever. Some of the square plates have to be cut to shape, but this is a very easy operation. We advise every dealer handling "Primus" to make himself a Tank at once. There can be no better form of advertising, both for himself and his shop, and it is certain that he is going to book big orders for sets. Once it is known that a model of the Tank is on view at So-and-so's, people will crowd to see it, and father will lose no time in buying a set of parts for his son (and incidentally for himself). We do not suppose that Messrs. Butcher can commence to send out models to their customers in the trade. They have several men working as hard as possible in erecting them, but the number turned out is not likely to satisfy even those who have succeeded in booking one for show purposes. We do not know if Messrs. Butcher intend to get out a special Tank set. We cannot imagine them failing to do so, as it will undoubtedly become a very big line, but of course, as each of their sets is designed to allow of the erection of a suitable number of different models, some little difficulty may be met with in arranging a set adhering to this principle. Still, we think the trade will want Tank sets, and so will the public.

It is undoubtedly a big triumph for "Primus" engineering, and we advise all dealers who think of building a Tank for themselves to write to Messrs. W. Butcher & Sons, Ltd., Camera House, Farringdon Avenue, London, E.C., who, we are sure, will do their utmost to supply them with a working design and particulars of the parts required. We understand they have a fairly large stock of the necessary sets in hand at the moment, and should be able to deliver by return.

20

By May, 1919, Whitanco announced their toys were in big demand. By February, 1920, they boasted of selling 1,100,000 mechanical toys and 500,000 non mechanical during 1919.

Whitanco 696 Locomotives

Whitanco 696 L&NWR Locomotive

Whitanco 696 GNR Locomotive

Clockwork Engine

F 17. **Clockwork Engine,** L. & N. W., G. N., and Midland Railway. Length 7¾ inches.
F 17. **Locomotive Mécanique,** Chemins de Fer L. & N. W., G. N., et Midland Railway. 19¾ cm. de longueur.
F 17. **Locomotora Mecánico,** Ferrocarriles L. & N. W., G. N. y Midland Railway. 19¾ cm de largo.
96/- per dozen

Railway Carriage and Truck

J 1. L. & N. W., G. N., and Midland Railway Carriage. 5¾ inches long.
J 1. Voiture des Chemins de fer L. & N. W., G. N., et Midland Railway. 14¼ cm. de longueur.
J 1. Coche de los Ferrocarriles L. & N. W., G. N., y Midland Railway. 14¼ cm. de largo.
23/- per dozen.

J 2. **Truck.**—L. & N. W., G. N., and Midland Railway Truck. 5¾ inches long.
J 2. **Truc**—Truc des Chemins de fer L. & N. W., G. N., et Midland Railway. 14¼ cm. de longueur.
J 2. **Carretón.**—Carretón de los Ferrocarriles L. & N. W., G. N. y Midland Railway. 14¼ cm. de largo.
19/- per dozen.

The Whitanco June 1920 advertisement stated they were now making 9,000 mechanical toys a day It showed their F1 set, comprising an engine, tender, two carriages and eight lengths of rail cost just 16/6 in old money (=£0.85p!). Their larger F2 set, with a brake van and ten lengths of rail 19/- (=£0.95p!).

They only showed these however in LNWR (black) livery and GNR (green) livery. So, imagine my surprise finding a MR (Midland Railway) set and carriages and trucks, thanks to Mr. Mike Cooke. Delivery of their train sets started in July, 1920.

These were the larger 7 ¾ inch (197mm) models and all had the cabside number – 696. This was incidentally their Liverpool, Anfield telephone number. The sets were clearly too expensive, so I wonder how many of their de-luxe complete train sets they sold at 50/- (£2.50). Perhaps it was an attempt to clear stocks?

Whitanco 696 MR Locomotive

The 696 Passenger Sets

Top row: LNWR No. 696 loco, tender, two coaches and Brake van.
Middle row: GNR No. 696 loco and tender. This has a replica electric 3-rail power unit as I only found a body shell and tender. The GNR coaches have Carette couplings - and may be Carette, from Whitanco tooling. I have never, ever seen such GNR coaches with the Whitanco logo in the centre.
Bottom row: The MR loco and tender is superb, as is the Whitanco MR coach. This is the only one I know in captivity, kindly loaned by Mr. Mike King. The MR Brake van is mine, coming from a freight set. The GNR Brake van just to balance the photograph.

The 696 Freight Sets

The F3 freight sets had just the locomotive, tender and two open wagons.
The F4 sets had the passenger guards van included as a brake van.

Whitanco made no other goods wagons.

The 333 Sets

To meet the challenge, they made in 1920 a superb, much smaller engine with the cabside number – 333. This was just 5 ¼ inch long (133mm) in Midland Railway maroon livery with matching carriages. As their larger brother, they were advertised as being available in LNWR colours, as well as GNR. To my knowledge, however, only the Midland version has ever been seen. They were brilliantly engineered, almost over engineered one could say. They made matching passenger carriages, brake vans and open trucks. The larger vehicles 5 ¾ inches long (146mm) while the smaller ones just 5 inches (127mm).

The MR loco No.333 with tender usually had just two coaches, but I found a third which looks better. Whitanco never made a Brake van for this smaller series. The smaller MR open wagon is the only one I have. In June, 1921, their 333 train sets were advertised at 21/- each (£1.05), but by 1923 they were reduced to 12/11d (£0.65). A reduction of 38 percent!

F 18. Clockwork Engine, L. & N. W., G. N., and Midland Railway. Length, 6 inches.

J 3. L. & N. W., G. N., and Midland Railway Carriage. 5 inches long.

J 4. Truck.—L. & N. W., G. N., and Midland Railway Truck. 5 inches long.

Boys! construct & run your own railroad

THE "WHITANCO" CLOCK-WORK TRAIN IS COMPLETE WITH 139 INTER-CHANGEABLE AND DETACHABLE PARTS WITH FULL EXPLANATORY DETAILS.

Price: 21/- each.
From all the Leading Toy Dealers.

Insist on seeing
This Trade Mark.

EVERY PART OF THE CLOCKWORK AND RAILWAY LINES CAN BE TAKEN APART AND RE-BUILT.

SPARE PARTS CAN BE OBTAINED FROM ALL THE LEADING TOY DEALERS.

THE "WHITANCO" CLOCK-WORK TRAIN IS THE MOST INSTRUCTIVE AND ABSORBING MODEL RAILWAY EVER PRODUCED.

Manufactured entirely at the Whitanco Works by—
WHITELEY, TANSLEY & CO., LTD., Dept. B.O.P., Beech Street, LIVERPOOL.

IF ANY DIFFICULTY IS FOUND IN OBTAINING THIS TRAIN SET FROM YOUR DEALERS, SEND A POSTCARD FOR PARTICULARS, GIVING YOUR FULL NAME AND ADDRESS

B.O.P. 11.] *When Buying anything Advertised in these pages please say that you saw the advertisement in the B.O.P.*

From Boy's Own Paper, 1921

The Rivals

The rivals in more ways than one! The LNWR and Midland Railway were fierce rivals, as were Whitanco and Meccano/Hornby in 1921.

The photograph shows the 333 Whitanco set racing the Hornby train to win the market share.

One of their innovations was their couplings. It had a realistic, telescopic effect that as the train pulled away, one carriage or truck started at a time, like the ripple effect of loose coupled stock on real railways. The only time I have seen this – ever – on model railways. Incidentally, they only made passenger brake vans, never goods brake vans. Their freight sets had two open wagons and the matching passenger brake van.

On top of this they produced their own tinplate track, points and diamond crossover. They introduced an ingenious track system of just components. You could purchase the rail, sleepers, pin etc., separately.

Railway Lines and Points

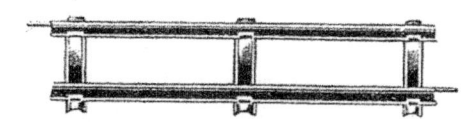

L 1. Straight Rails, Gauge 0. = 1⅜".
L 1. Rails Droits, largeur entre les Rails, 1 cm de longueur.
L 1. Carriles Derechos, anchura entre los Carriles, 1 cm. de largo.
7/- per dozen.

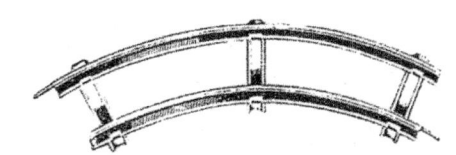

L 2. Curved Rails, Guage 0. = 1⅜".
L 2. Rails Courbés, largeur entre les Rails, 1 cm. de longueur.
L 2. Carriles Encorvados, anchura entre los Carriles, 1 cm. de largo.
7/- per dozen.

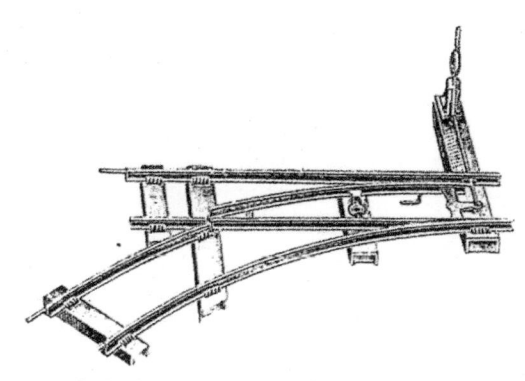

L 4. Left-hand Switch Point.
L 4. Aiguille à Gauche.
L 4. Aguja á la Izquierda.
26/- per dozen.

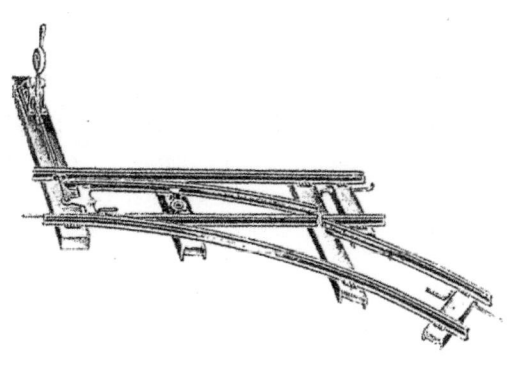

L 3. Right-hand Switch Point.
L 3. Aiguille à Droite.
L 3. Aguja á la Derecha.
26/- per dozen

Whitanco Accessories

Item D1 was a station, measuring 16 inches (410mm) long by 4 inches (100mm) wide. It was identical in style to the Carette English railway station, No. 918. This measured 23 inches long (584mm) by 5 inches wide (127mm).

No. 918
English Railway Station

handsomely made and nicely japanned, 23" long, 5" wide each 3/-

Could Whitanco have produced the tool for this Carette station above before the war in 1912?

Item D2 (right) was a beautiful two part footbridge, with two signals. A lovely piece, 18 ½ inches long (467mm). This took ages to identify and find.

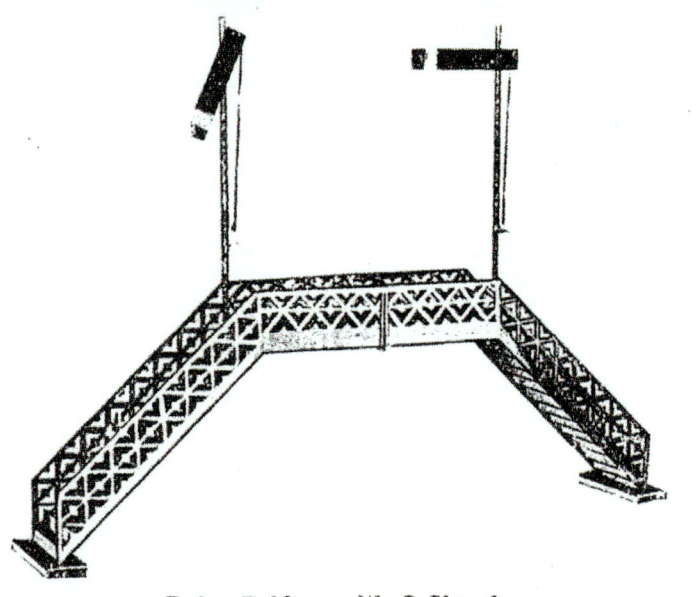

D 2. Bridge, with 2 Signals, total length, 18½ inches

A page from a Whitanco catalogue of around 1920 headed 'Railway Outfits', showing an L&NWR clockwork train on lines, a station and a bridge with signals. The unusual thing about this set is that the station looks like a Bing 'Victoria Station' from the same period, rather than the Whitanco 'Richmond Station'. Was there a link with Bing?

Railway Outfits.

F 5. **Clockwork Train on Lines,** L. & N. W., G. N., and Midland Railway Engine, 2 Coaches, Guard's Van, 10 Lines, Station, Bridge with Signals. 30 inches long.

F 5. **Chemin de Fer,** Mécanique, L. & N. W., G. N., et Midland Railway Locomotive, 2 Voitures, Fourgon, 10 Rails, Gare, Pont à Signaux. 76½ cm. de longueur.

F 5. **Camino de Hierro,** Mecánico, L. & N. W., G. N., y Midland Railway Locomotora, 2 Coches, Coche del Guarda, 10 Lineas, Estación, Puente de Señales. 76½ cm. de largo.

360/- per dozen.

Item D3, I am guessing, because it was not shown in the catalogue, was a double skin tunnel, Measuring 7 ¾ inches (196mm) long by 6 ¾ inches (170mm) wide by 6 inches (150mm) tall. The weird thing is you look inside and it is made from surplus tinprinted sheets of the MR Tender!

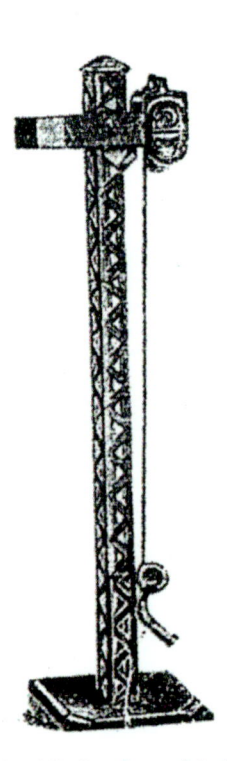

D 4. Signal, 13 inches high, with lamp to light.
D 4. Signal.
D 4. Señal.
38/- per dozen.

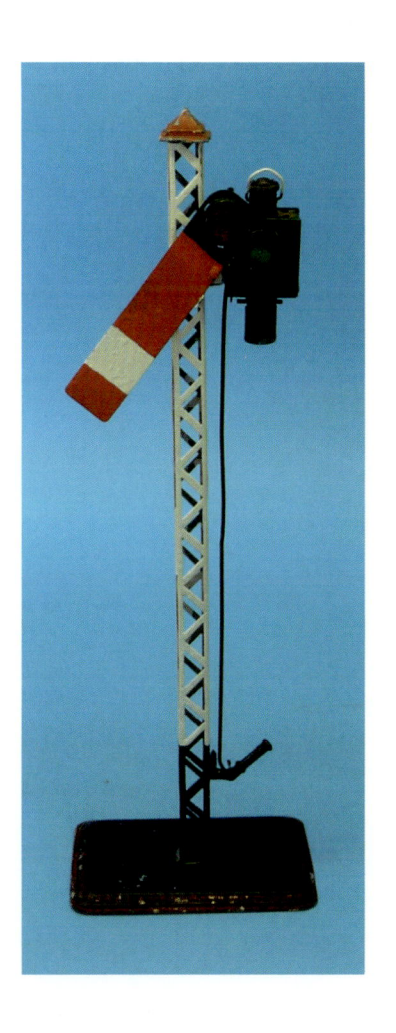

Finally, D4 (centre) is a signal, 13 inches (330mm) tall which is identical to the Carette No. 647/200 (right) shown in their 1912 catalogue.

Could it be old Carette stock, as they went out of business in 1917?

There is no doubt that Whitanco were an innovative, energetic company, well lead but tragically eclipsed by the post war financial turmoil.

The March issue, 1920 of Games and Toys reported Mr. Ernest Whiteley had been elected to be Vice Chairman of the Association of Toy Manufacturers, stating. . . 'he was a keen fighter and brilliant speaker.' In 1923 they went on to say. . . 'no person had done more for the development of the British toy industry.'

Their sales figures and payroll costs tell their own story:-

21/07/1922 to 20/01/1923   sales were £29,665.00   against payroll costs of £19,094.00

21/01/1923 to 20/07/1923   "   "   £34,723.00   "   "   "   " £31,133.00

21/07/1923 to 20/01/1924   "   "   £36,172.00   "   "   "   " £35,660.00

21/01/1924 to 20/07/1924   "   "   £36,934.00   "   "   "   " £35,822.00

21/07/1924 to 02/12/1924   "   "   £36,952.00   "   "   "   " not recorded

Sadly, on the 20th July, 1921, a Mr. George Leather, an accountant of 24, North John Street, Liverpool was brought in as Receiver/manager. They struggled on, but finally stopped trading on the 2nd December, 1924, the financial dissolvement being completed on 3rd May, 1929.

However, this is not the end of the story.

Mr. Ernest Whiteley joined forces with a major toy distributor in the region – G.E Garnett and Sons Ltd., who had been in business for 70 years. They were a wholesale house, founded in 1826 and commenced buying toys in 1890. Garnett, Whiteley Ltd was registered on the 19th July, 1923. Quoting the Games and Toys article. . .'They are mechanical and consulting engineers, machinists, fitters and toolmakers, manufacturers of telegraphic and telephonic instruments, toys and instruments of science and precision.' They were based at the Lotus Works in Broad Green Road, Liverpool 13 in a 10,000 square foot factory with the most up to date plant and machinery. This was the site of the old Lotus Laundry Company. They changed their name to the Lotus Radio Company in 1933 and continued making tuning condensers and the like up to the Second World War. They were dissolved in 1942. All records sadly destroyed in The Public Records Offices in Kew by the 21 year rule on the 8th August, 1963.

The tools of the old Whitanco company were transferred to Garnett, Whiteley Ltd., and in turn, sold to Burnett Ltd. Burnett themselves were merchants only, buying and selling a wide range of toys.

Founded in 1914, it is widely thought, though not yet proven, that their toys were made by the famous Barringer, Wallis and Manners Ltd., long established tin printers later formed into the Metal Box Co.

I have samples of the Whitanco carpet train, now in LMS and LNER livery with the Burnett trademark clearly printed. This must be in the late 1920's, say 1926 or 1927.

GARNETT'S OF LIVERPOOL
Celebrate Centenary

The Founder George Edmund Garnett

Not very many businesses in the toy trade can claim a hundred years of history, and it is therefore something of an event when one celebrates its centenary.

The firm of G. E. Garnett & Sons, Ltd., the well-known Liverpool wholesale house, had its hundredth birthday last month. Although it was not until 1926 that it became a limited company, Garnett's was first established in Richmond Row, Liverpool, by George Edmund Garnett in 1854—the year of the outbreak of the Crimean War.

Garnett's history is a family story—the story of a business passing from father to son through successive generations, and of sons and grandsons—bearing invariably the christian names of their predecessors—carrying on the firm's proud traditions.

The first George Garnett, the founder, was eventually joined by his two sons—George the Second and William the First. After the death of the founder, the two sons carried on the business so successfully that, at the turn of the century, larger premises were acquired at the junction of St. Anne Street and Islington, Liverpool—premises which have extended even further along Islington with the continual development of this pioneer house.

As far back as 1890, the second George Garnett was a buyer at the Manchester Toy Fair. In 1892, his brother William began to visit the January Fairs with him, and from that time on, the Garnett brothers became familiar figures at the Manchester shows.

In course of time there were four Garnetts to be seen at the Manchester Fairs—and subsequently at Leeds and Harrogate. For George the Second had been joined by his son George the Third, and William had been joined by

The Late George Garnett.

The Late William Garnett.

his son William the Second.

When the elder William passed away in 1951, he was greatly missed by his brother George, who was undoubtedly deeply affected. George outlived his brother by only two years, passing away last year in his eightieth year. In characteristic fashion, he died in his office.

35

An even bigger surprise was finding some pressed steel '0' gauge track, straights and curves, printed 'GW and Co.' and a patent pending number. This eluded me for years, until the very helpful team in the Patent Records Offices in High Holborn, London found the original patent. This showed the patent was lodged on the 1st March, 1923 by Mr. Ernest Whiteley himself and granted on the 1st July, 1924. Too late for Whitanco Ltd., but clearly Garnett, Whiteley Ltd.

Whether it was sold by them or not, I do not know, but again, the tools were transferred to Burnett Ltd., to resurface twenty five years later as the pressed steel track of Chad Valley Ltd. in 1948. This time with points, crossovers etc., included.

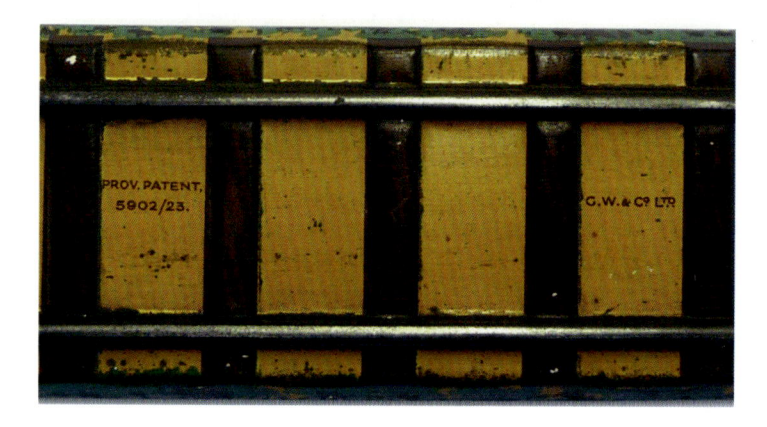

PATENT SPECIFICATION

217,959

Application Date: March 1, 1923. No. 5902/23.

Complete Left: Dec. 3, 1923.

Complete Accepted: July 1, 1924.

PROVISIONAL SPECIFICATION.

Improvements in or relating to Toy Railway Lines.

I, ERNEST WHITELEY, (British), of Kinreen, Allerton Drive, Mossley Hill, Liverpool, in the County of Lancaster, do hereby declare the nature of this invention to be as follows:—

This invention relates to toy railway lines, and has for its objects to provide a line which may be cheaply constructed and shall be of pleasing appearance.

In carrying out my invention, a "permanent way" or base portion, "sleepers", and upstanding rails of a line section or component are formed by means of suitable pressure tools out of or from a single piece of sheet metal.

The sides of said base members are bent to form walls or flanges which are preferably outwardly inclined somewhat, and the lower edges whereof may be inturned or beaded; thus the line is raised from its table, floor, or other support.

Said sleepers are formed by jumped or raised transverse portions of the base arranged at spaced intervals, and the rails are produced by parallel ∩ lengths extending longitudinally of the base.

As means for detachably connecting together adjacent line sections or components, metal pins or spindles may be provided at one end of each section, a portion of each pin being permanently secured—without the aid of solder, or the like—within an end of a rail, the outer or free portion of the pin being adapted to be inserted into the pinless end of a rail of the next adjacent line section.

To secure a pin in part in the end of a rail the metal of the latter around or below the pin may be squeezed or forced inwardly during the process of manufacture, to clinch the pin in position, or a portion or portions of the base adjacent to the rail may be so severed that a tongue piece or tongue pieces is or are created, which tongue or tongues is or are adapted to be forced around the nearby portion of the pin.

The fastening of a pin may be effected at intervals of its length, if desired.

In a modified construction, the line sections may be secured to a wooden or like base board or plate, on one end whereof there are provided integral dovetailed or like projections, and at the other end are formed recesses of corresponding shape or configuration; the line sections are detachably secured together by the engagement of the end projections of one section into the appropriate recess of the next adjacent section.

The line is preferably painted, the base portion of one colour and the sleepers of another colour.

Dated this 27th day of February, 1923.

JOHN HINDLEY WALKER,
139, Dale Street, Liverpool.
Registered Patent Agent.

Obviously, radio was 'THE' thing in the immediate post war years. Introduced in 1919, Dame Nellie Melba made her first broadcast on the 15th June, 1920, from Chelmsford, singing 'The Australian Nightingale.' In 1922, tuning in to '240 Savoy Hill' was the norm till, on the 14th May, 1932, it moved to Broadcasting House, Portland Place, London.

The post war prosperity collapsed 1918 – 1920 which led to high unemployment. The market conditions were just against such a new venture. Such was the energy and entrepreneurship of Ernest Whiteley and his colleagues, they recognised the new market of radio and changed direction.

Their toys were brilliant, beautifully engineered. It is funny how markets differ – a Whitanco locomotive could fetch £150.00 or more in good condition today, yet their motor bus or char-a-banc at least £1,500.00 or more. A clever company indeed, whose products deserve recognition and respect. Their quality was very good, substantial and full of charm.

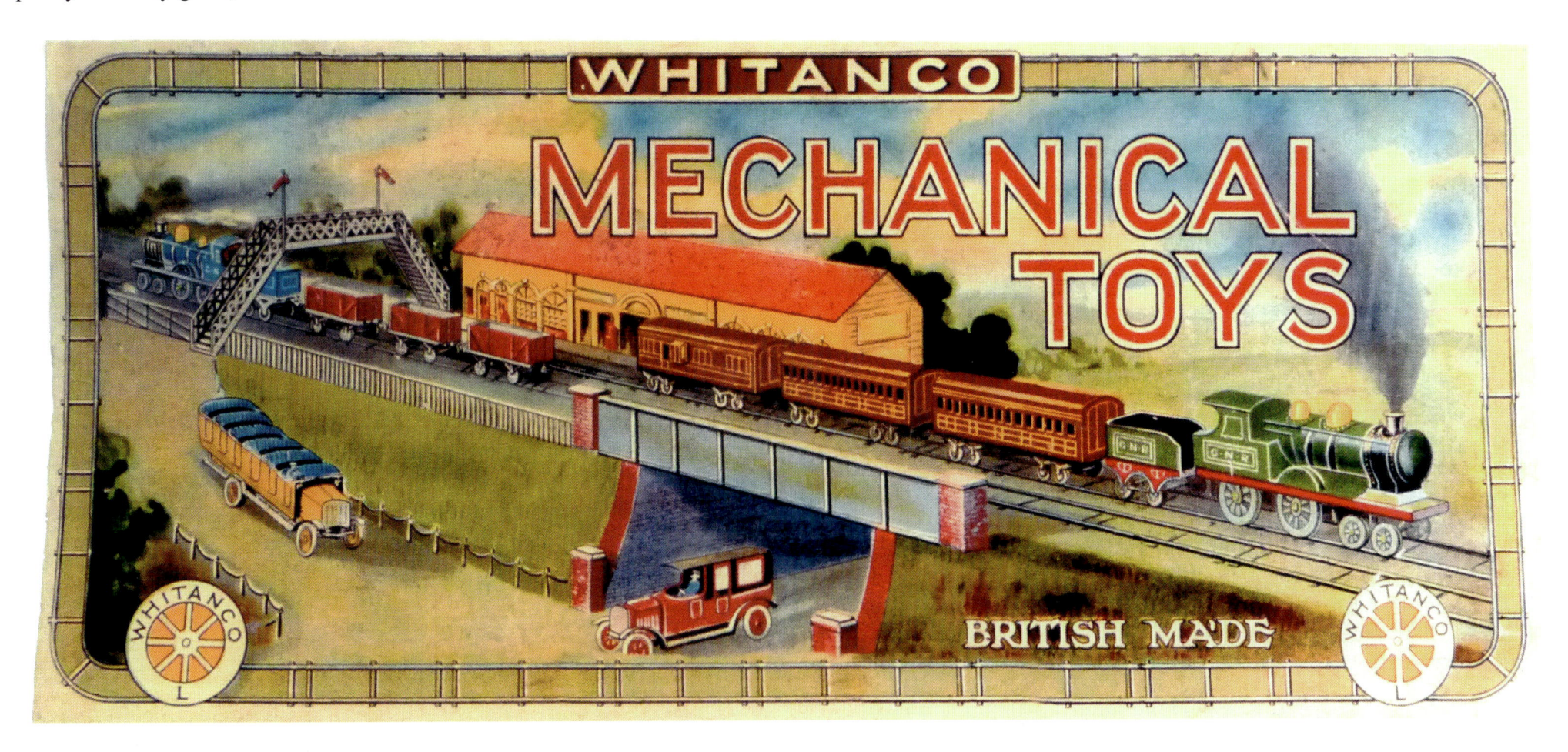

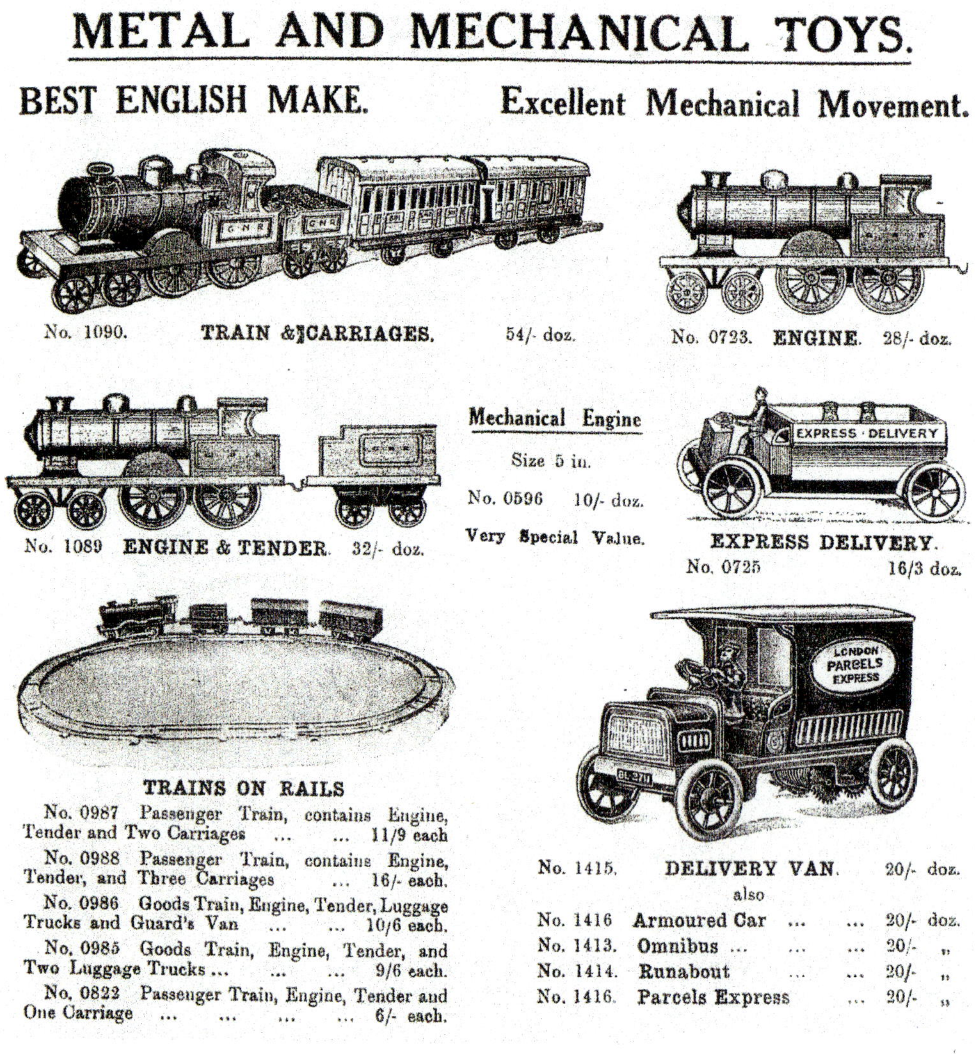

METAL AND MECHANICAL TOYS.

BEST ENGLISH MAKE.   Excellent Mechanical Movement.

No. 1090.   TRAIN & CARRIAGES.   54/- doz.

No. 0723.   ENGINE.   28/- doz.

No. 1089.   ENGINE & TENDER.   32/- doz.

Mechanical Engine
Size 5 in.
No. 0596   10/- doz.
Very Special Value.

EXPRESS DELIVERY.
No. 0725   16/3 doz.

TRAINS ON RAILS

No. 0987 Passenger Train, contains Engine, Tender and Two Carriages ... ... 11/9 each

No. 0988 Passenger Train, contains Engine, Tender, and Three Carriages ... 16/- each.

No. 0986 Goods Train, Engine, Tender, Luggage Trucks and Guard's Van ... ... 10/6 each.

No. 0985 Goods Train, Engine, Tender, and Two Luggage Trucks ... ... 9/6 each.

No. 0822 Passenger Train, Engine, Tender and One Carriage ... ... 6/- each.

No. 1415.   DELIVERY VAN.   20/- doz.
also
No. 1416   Armoured Car ... ... 20/- doz.
No. 1413.   Omnibus ... ... 20/- ,,
No. 1414.   Runabout ... ... 20/- ,,
No. 1416.   Parcels Express ... ... 20/- ,,

Extract from an unknown retailers catalogue, featuring Whitanco toys. The model vehicles at the bottom right are believed to be by Burnett Ltd.

The Burnett Co. Ltd.

The Burnett Co. Ltd.

This company was a very famous and successful supplier of tin printed toys throughout the 1920's and 1930's.

Mrs Marguerite Fawdry, in her marvellous book –"British Tin Toys", published by New Cavendish Books, gave some interesting details on the company. For those of you who do not know this book, it is a virtual A-Z and encyclopaedia of British toy manufacturers. Indeed, New Cavendish Books set such a superlative standard in their histories of many toy manufacturers.
She writes: " The company was registered on the 3rd October, 1914, as manufacturers of mechanical and automatic toys and novelties," their directors being Mr. F.Burnett and Mr. E.Satchwell." They were based at 11, Grosvenor Buildings, Steelhouse Lane, Birmingham. Their London offices were first at 52, Aldersgate Street, before moving around the corner to 21/23, Chiswell Street, EC1 in 1934.

They were merchants, that is wholesale traders only, not actual manufacturers. I do not know where the entrepreneurship originated, as Mrs Fawdry thinks the toys were made by Barringer, Wallis and Manners Ltd., a highly skilled family firm of tinprinters. Did Burnett Ltd., commission the models, or did BWM Ltd., produce them and had Burnett Co. Ltd. sell them?

BWM's origins date back to 1830. They started making tins in 1889 and became Barringer, Wallis and Manners Ltd., in 1892. They certainly had the skill to print and make these toys, simplistic though they were, but so did Hudson, Scott Ltd of Carlisle who I mentioned in my opening sentences. It is felt the toy car advertised in Games and Toys in November, 1914, was made by BWM Ltd. They had responded to the plea by the British Board of Trade in the Summer of 1914 for British companies to fill the gap left by the near monopoly of the Nuremberg manufacturers. However, the very first British made motor cars, vans, omnibuses etc., came out with the distinctive Burnett trademark and are highly prized today.

Trains were missing originally, but this entrepreneurship had them negotiate and buy the old Whitanco tools from Garnett, Whiteley Co. Ltd., as they changed direction from toy manufacture to making radio sets. This must have been around 1925.

The first model was an impressive, red carpet loco and tender, cab side No. 1066 (below) but soon the tender was dropped and an LMS and LNER version of the loco only came out in 1928. They stayed in production till 1936.

Burnett introduced their famous constructional "Ubilda" range of toys in 1932.

Their really quite attractive 4-4-2 Tank engine in LMS and LNE livery, No. 11861 came out in 1934. It had 30 separate parts and cost just 2/6d (£0.13).

The models were well made indeed and included in the set was a little envelope complete with key and a spanner. They were let down by their poor, one could say pathetic wire spring clockwork mechanisms. As I was told by old employees at Metal Box in Mansfield, who took over BWM in 1939, they were tin printers, not mechanical engineers.

UBILDA
YOU BUILD IT
UBILDA
MADE IN ENGLAND
30 SEPARATE PARTS FOR MAKING A MECHANICALLY PROPELLED AIR LINER
AIR LINER
UBILDA
YOU BUILD IT
LOCO
30 SEPARATE PARTS FOR MAKING A MECHANICAL LOCOMOTIVE
LNER
LILLIPUT ENGINE (MECHANICAL)
LNER
11861
17841
L M S
LMS

1934 Catalogue

I came across their 1934 catalogue which I reproduce here, to go with the beautiful reprint Mrs. Fawdry put in her book of the 1935-1936 catalogue, found in the archives of a Toy importer in India!

Page 9

UBILDA LOCOMOTIVE
(No. 104/30)
(No. 105/30)

Further contributions to the outfit of youthful Railway enthusiasts.

Sturdy models in two decorations, i.e.
L.M.S. — RED.
L.N.E. — GREEN.

Fitted with strong clockwork mechanism.

The building and running of these Engines will be an endless source of amusement.

30 parts to this fine toy.

When built-up, overall dimensions :—
10" × 2¼" × 1¾"

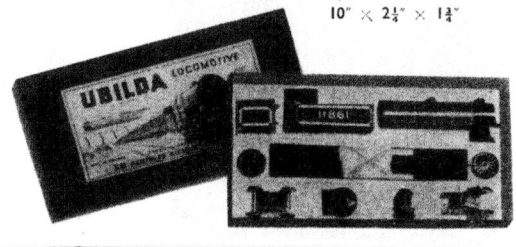

Burnett's for "Ubilda"

Page 28

ENGINE
(No. 24/12)

Popular all the year round.

A splendid carpet toy, in familiar L. M. & S. or L. N. E. colours, i.e., Red or Green, with distinctive lettering.

Length 8 inches.

Burnett's for Mechanical Toys

Page 33

ENGINE
(No. 17/6)

A strong mechanical toy of bright appearance.

Decorated in colours of either L. M. & S. and L. & N. E., i.e., red or green., with distinctive lettering.

Length 5 inches.

MONOPLANE
(No. 83/6)

Bright red and yellow decorations

This strong up-to-date model enjoys wide popularity.

The mechanism drives the plane and the propellor rotates.

Length 8½ inches.

Burnett's for Mechanical Toys

44

UBILDA Royal Scot

1935 saw the release of their beautiful "Royal Scot" engine and tender. Remember, these are carpet toys, yet the detail and printing made them a worthy, accurate model, even if a fraction over size! Some seven percent larger than an '0' gauge model. It really is an impressive engine. You could not set it on '0' gauge track, but by adding a couple of washers on the bogie axles, she fits well on Gauge 1 track (45mm). The box picture and instructions inside the lid must have made this a popular toy. It is all about imagination.

The set had 68 separate parts to be assembled, following detailed instructions inside the box lid. (See page 47)

UBILDA Royal Scot box and instructions

Page 2

UBILDA LOCOMOTIVE
(Nos. 99/90 & 103/90)

Wonderful models of the World's most famous Railway Engines.

L.M.S. ROYAL SCOT.
L.N.E. FLYING SCOTSMAN.

Decorated in authentic colours. Fitted with strong clockwork motor.

The gem of the Ubilda range of constructional toys.

An engineering lesson.
A splendid toy.

The 68 parts build up into a Locomotive overall dimensions :—18" × 2½" × 4"

Burnett's for "Ubilda"

UBILDA
LOCOMOTIVE
ROYAL SCOT

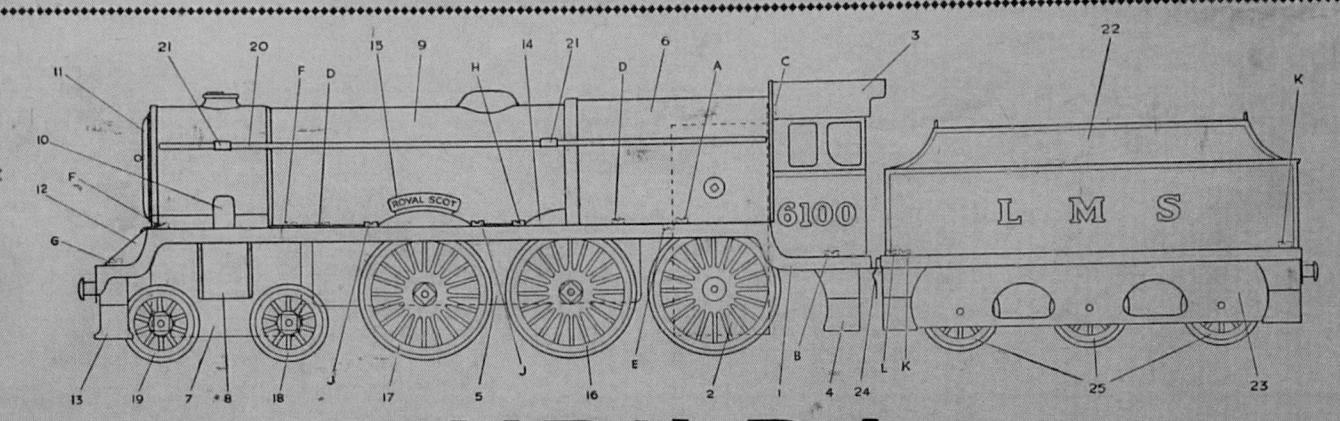

68 PARTS TO BUILD A ROYAL SCOT LOCOMOTIVE

INSTRUCTIONS

The instructions for building the Locomotive should be followed and the parts assembled in the order stated. Numbers on the diagram refer to parts of the Locomotive, while letters indicate the bolts and nuts which fix them.

Commence with the main Frame (1) and Mechanism (2) with a pair of driving wheels attached. Push the Mechanism through the Frame from the under side. If you just press the spring in slightly it will pass through the slot in Frame quite easily.

Fix with bolts (A).

The Cab (3) is next fastened to the Frame with bolts (B), and at the same time fix the Steps (4). From inside the cab put in bolt (C). This will also pass through tab on the Mechanism. Put nut on but do not screw up tightly yet.

Next the Driving Wheel Chassis (5) is fixed with slot towards mechanism. Bolts (D).

Now take the Fire Box (6) and hook the top tab on bolt (C), then fix to frame by bolts (E). Bolt (C) can now be screwed up tight.

Bogie Chassis (7) and Cylinders (8) come next. Insert the bottom tab of the Cylinders in the slot on side of Chassis, then hook the other tab into the slot on top. This unit will then appear as shown in Fig. 1, and should be fixed to the front part of frame with bolts (F), taking care that the two slots in frame and chassis correspond.

Continue building by inserting the end of Boiler (9) into the opening in Fire Box (6). Now put the tab ends of the Exhaust Tubes (10) into the holes in frame just over the Cylinders (8) with the projecting tabs pointing outwards. Carefully adjust the Boiler so that the upper ends of Exhaust tubes enter their respective holes.

The Boiler End (11) comes next. Hook the small tab into the slot on top of Boiler, place the Frame Bracket (12) in position and bring the bottom part of Boiler End down so that it fits properly over the Boiler. Put bolt 9 through the holes and slip on the front Steps (13) before putting on the nut. Screw up tight.

Proceed by fixing the Half Wheel Guards (14) with bolts (H) and the Wheel Guards (15) by bolts (J).

The Model is now ready for the Wheels. First place one of the Driving Wheels (16) in position, push axle through as far as the hole on other side of chassis. Put the other wheel in its place and push the axle right through. Screw on nut. Repeat this operation for the other Driving Wheels (17). It is now a very simple matter to fix the four Bogie Wheels (18) and (19) with the other two axles and nuts.

Complete this part of the Locomotive by sliding the Hand Rails (20) through the two Brackets (21).

The Tender should now be built by first fixing the Body (22) to the Chassis (23) by means of four bolts (K).

Fix the Coupling Hook (24) by pushing through the slot in end of Chassis and fasten with bolt (L).

To assemble the Wheels (25) of the tender. Take one of the axles, slip a wheel on each end, insert one end through hole in side of chassis from the inside. Now bring the other end of axle over the hole when it will spring in. Repeat this for the other four wheels.

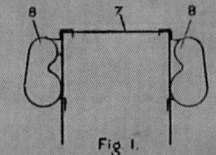

Fig. 1.

If you have followed the instructions given above the "UBILDA" model Locomotive is now complete.

BURNETT LTD · LONDON

The Lilliput Engine

In the 1935/6 catalogue, they list, but do not show, a companion to the LMS Royal Scot – "The Flying Scotsman" of the LNER. Wow! It must have been superb. I have never actually seen one, or come across anyone who has. Did it ever reach production? I simply do not know. As with the other toys we have mentioned, the cars, vans, buses, aeroplanes achieve much higher prices today than the locomotives. There was really not much you could do with them. Wind them up and they might go half way across the carpet!

It was all about price, I am sure, so perhaps these top of the range models were too expensive. The same 1935/6 catalogue introduces a baby clockwork engine they called the Lilliput engine, just 5 inches long (127mm) in both LNER and LMS liveries. Again the wire spring clockwork mechanisms let them down, but they were so cheap.

Burnett Ltd., closed in 1940. A coincidence as Barringer, Wallis and Manners Ltd., too were finally taken over by Metal Box Ltd., the same year and production closed. Did Burnett close because their supplier stopped production, or visa versa? I do not know.

Once again, Chad Valley Ltd in the late 1930's, hungry to get into the metal toy market and copy the incredible success of Meccano Ltd., arranged a source of tinplate soon after VE Day (Victory in Europe) in 1944 and took over the Burnett tools. They were the first on the market in 1946 and had enormous success initially. They quickly realised the weakness of the wire spring mechanisms and fitted their own much more sophisticated, stronger mechanisms.

In 1948, Chad Valley produced their own model railway system, a real quality product, strong and reliable giving immense play value. I know, I had a Chad Valley layout as a boy but more of this later.

The Burnett toys were beautifully produced, printed and sold well, making them so popular with collectors today.

UBILDA
REGISTERED

YOU BUILD IT

LOCO

30 SEPARATE PARTS FOR MAKING A MECHANICAL LOCOMOTIVE

Ubilda Fire Engine
(No. 66/30).
Retail price **2/6**

Working model of Fire Engine in parts, 10ins. long with extending ladder. In box 9¼ins. × 9¼ins. × 2ins.

Ubilda Loco.
No. 58/30).
Retail price **2/6**

Metal parts to build a working model of Locomotive, 10ins. long. In box 10¼ins. × 8ins. × 2ins.

50

The Chad Valley Trains

The Chad Valley Trains

What a company! As their 1954 catalogue put it - "Internationally known as one of the most famous manufacturers of toys and games in existence". They were a huge manufacturer of quality stationers sundries and wooden games and toys. They had such a sound reputation and sales throughout the UK and British Dominion. They had over 8,000 customers in the mid 1950's.

The business was founded in 1860 by brothers Joseph and Alfred Johnson at 7-9, George Street, Birmingham. In 1897 they transferred to their new model factory in Chad Valley, Harborne, Birmingham. I have to hand an interesting article written by Mr. Alfred Johnson on the 18th September, 1919:
"The future prospects of the company and it's programme for further erection of new buildings and plant are temporarily rendered uncertain by the unexpected action of the Government in admitting the free importing of German and Austrian toys into this country in contravention of everything which the toy manufacturers here have been led to expect. Whether the Government's hypothesis that "Germany has very few toys to sell and is not in a favourable position to produce them now" - has any substantial basis in fact or not is difficult to say. Undoubtedly, the effect of the removal of restrictions has been a loss of confidence in the Government's intention to protect a new industry which was almost entirely a foreign one and which is not yet sufficiently well established here to be able to withstand open competition with the Nuremberg toy makers. The result is that wholesale and retail toy dealers are withholding their orders because they are uncertain what will happen and both buyers and sellers feel that the future prospects are too unreliable to offer inducements for further speculation and extensions to new buildings and plant".

In the 1920's, the latest steam locomotives were the 'Concordes' of their day. We had just had the amalgamation of all the railway companies into the 'Big Four'- The LMS, LNER, SR and GWR. The GWR had a very enthusiastic and go-ahead Publicity Department. To publicise their new 'Caerphilly Castle' locomotive, on show at the Empire Exhibition in Wembley in 1924, they commissioned Chad Valley to produce a promotional wooden jigsaw puzzle. So successful was this promotion, they sold 77,686 copies by the time the jigsaw was withdrawn in 1928. This led to the whole range of the famous 'Chad Valley' jigsaws for the GWR and other famous brands like Cunard and Dunlop.

In 1931 they took over Peacock Co. Ltd., a much respected and long established manufacturer of wooden toys. The 1935 Chad Valley catalogue featured another GWR engine. This time a full length pull-along train, made up of a King Class locomotive "King George V" and six carriages. It was almost '00' scale, beautifully detailed printed paper on wood with bead wheels. Catalogue reference P1440, priced at just 5/- (£0.25p), it is a rare toy to find today.

This was followed in 1936 by a quite superb Gauge One size (10mm to the foot) model of again "King George V". It was made of wood and printed paper and called the 'Runaway Train'. You pulled and released a string and the engine would run across the floor. The 1936 catalogue showed two versions. A smaller one, just 12 inches (300mm) long costing 3/11 (£0.20p) which I have never seen and the larger one I have, being 21 ½ inches (550mm), costing 5/6 (£0.27p). It really is the most wonderful model.

My company printers once sent me a Christmas card with a very evocative cover, showing a child taking a large toy engine out of a stocking. My brother and I had pillow cases at the end of our parent's bed!

Fast forward 60 years and a dear friend Brian Wright and his charming wife Margaret called on us one morning for coffee. Brian runs the annual Radley Windup near Abingdon, but is perhaps best known as Mr. Cat Graphics. He is a quite superb artist, making coach sides for Ace Trains and the like. We were chatting when Margaret mentioned she had such an engine when she was just six years old and had a photograph to prove it. I was able to bring down my engine and re-live the moment.

Chad Valley were having enormous success. Justifiably so as their product quality and service was fantastic. They even took the entire front page of the Daily Mail newspaper on the 22nd November, 1935 to advertise their wares.

They were so proud to receive a - 'by Royal Appointment' accolade from HM Queen Elizabeth, the Queen Mother in 1938

In the August, 1945 issue, Chad Valley showed for the first time their famous picture of children playing with their train set, looking out of the window at a GWR express rushing past the horizon. Their priority was export sales which started in December, 1945. Domestic sales following in early 1946. They used the Burnett tools for two years or more before new tools could be made. Production runs of 50,000 to 100,000 units were being produced of each model. They soon topped the £1,000,000 mark in sales turnover. An incredible sum in those days!

Games & Toys Vol.57 No.379 July 1945

MECHANICAL TOYS

ANNOUNCING FOR WINTER DELIVERY A COMPREHENSIVE RANGE COMPRISING:—
- CLOCKWORK DRIVEN AND OTHER PULL-ALONG TOYS
- HUMMING TOPS
- MONEY AND CASH BOXES
- ENGINES & MOTOR CARS INCLUDING "BURNETT" MODELS

FOR **HOME** AND **EXPORT**

BY APPOINTMENT TO H.M. THE QUEEN

THE CHAD VALLEY CO. LTD
HARBORNE
ENGLAND

Games & Toys Vol.57 No.380 August 1945

"UBILDA"

LOCOMOTIVE • FORT • MOTOR CAR
AND OTHER
MECHANICAL & PULL ALONG TOYS
FOR
WINTER DELIVERY

BY APPOINTMENT TOYMAKERS TO HER MAJESTY THE QUEEN

THE CHAD VALLEY CO. LTD
HARBORNE
ENGLAND

Major Roger Swinburne Johnson on being de-mobbed was appointed to the Board of Chad Valley in the Summer of 1947. Tragically, he had lost his two brothers in the War – Richard in the R.A.F. and Anthony in the Navy both in 1942. In November, 1947, the editor of Games and Toys was taken around the factories of Chad Valley by Major F.R.B Whitehouse MBE managing director and Major Swinburne Johnson. One of the factories visited was C. and G. Gauges Ltd., of High Haddon Works, Old Hill, Staffordshire who made clockwork units for mechanical toys by the thousand. Some 80,000 units a week! He learnt they were about to make a heavy gauge train set of, to quote - "The first quality".

There is a rumour – not nailed down – that C. and G. Gauges made clockwork mechanisms for the smaller Hornby trains from Meccano Ltd., too. The mechanisms for both Hornby and Chad Valley are identical, save the brake lever only. Who knows?

Major F.R.B Whitehouse MBE, approaching his retirement in 1956, wrote a fascinating article in the June issue, 1954, of Games and Toys on his memories of 40 years as a toy maker.

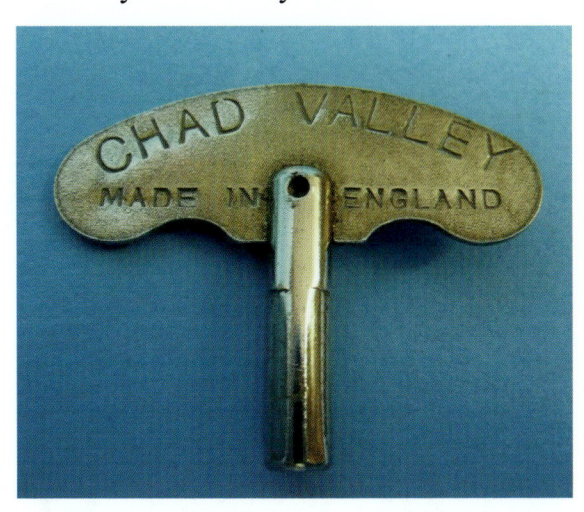

Would anyone have a copy of the brochure mentioned in the advert on the right?

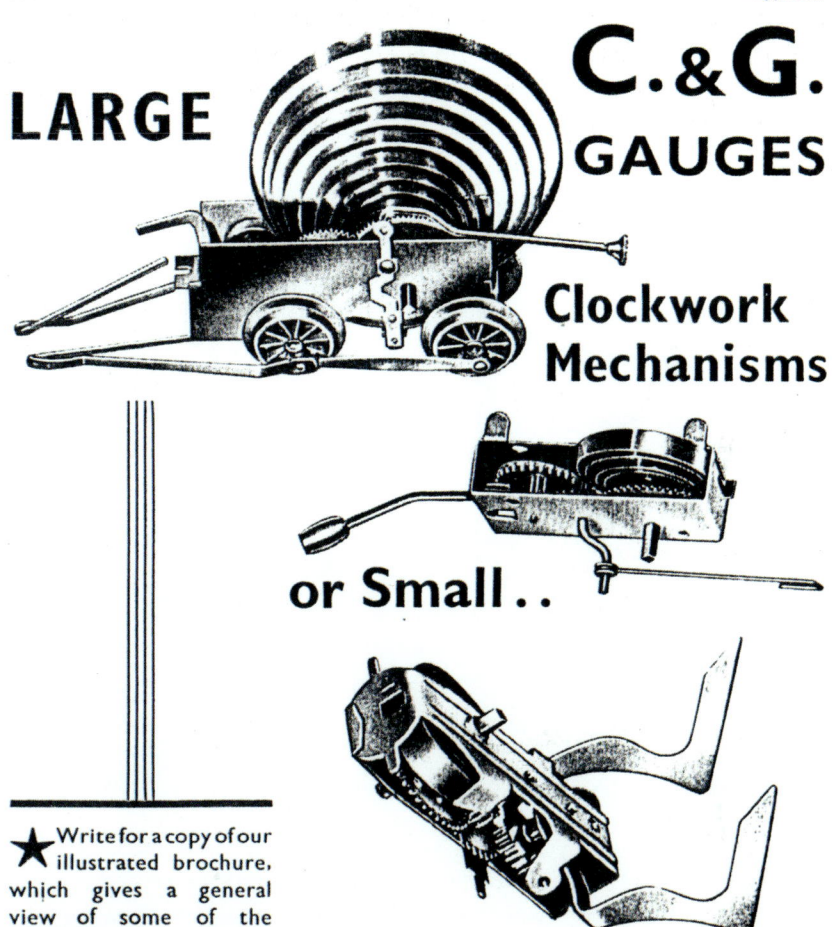

LARGE

C. & G. GAUGES

Clockwork Mechanisms

or Small..

★ Write for a copy of our illustrated brochure, which gives a general view of some of the mechanisms we produce

WE specialise in the production of clockwork mechanisms in all sizes and to extreme precision limits of ·0002. Our works are also well equipped to deal with special mechanisms made to our clients' own particular requirements. Every enquiry is treated confidentially and has our prompt attention

C. & G. GAUGES LTD.

HIGH HADEN WORKS • OLD HILL • STAFFORDSHIRE

Telephone: Halesowen 1624-5

1947 Catalogue

However, we go too fast. Trade catalogues were usually issued in January to coincide with the main Toy Fairs. The 1946 Chad Valley catalogue simply showed their games, jigsaws and dolls.

The 1947 catalogues showed the wonderful 10 inch (254mm) Large Bus, No. 10045 and the famous Delivery Van, No. 10032. There was a shortage of tinplate in 1948, so these models are frequently found made in aluminium.

The 5 inch loco, an exact copy of the Burnett toy also appeared as No. 10000, as did the Ubilda 4-4-2 Tank engine No. 10010. These cost 97/- a dozen, 8/- each (£0.40p).

One anomaly in the 1947 catalogue was the mention of 'An Electric Train Set', No. 10055, the next number up from a Ubilda vehicle under the 'Metal Toys' section. It did state details not yet available, but I have never seen it mentioned anywhere else, so believe it never made it through to production. No, it is not the 'Merlin' engine which was to follow five years later. Does anyone know what this was?

The Original Trains of 1948

Chad Valley launched their new train sets by a lovely colour advertisement on the front cover of Games and Toys in November, 1948. They only had two sets initially, Set 10063 being their famous 3402, 0-4-0 loco, tender and two coaches in Southern green and LMS red colour. The Southern green coaches had 'London – Southampton' as printed destination boards, while the LMS had 'Royal Scot'. The freight sets, No. 10067 were identical but with two open wagons in matching green and red with a large C V printed like private owner wagons.

Set 10063 (1948)

No. 10000C Locomotive of 1949

I mentioned earlier about the very poor wire spring mechanism fitted to the Burnett toys. Chad Valley recognised this, so in 1949, they brought out an uprated version. The original No. 10000 model is now the Mark 1 version, selling at 33/- a dozen = 2/9d each = £0.13p). The uprated model is now the No. 10000C, Mark IV, selling at 63/- a dozen = 5/4d each = £0.26p) This had the Chad Valley chimney and a much better mechanism which actually worked!

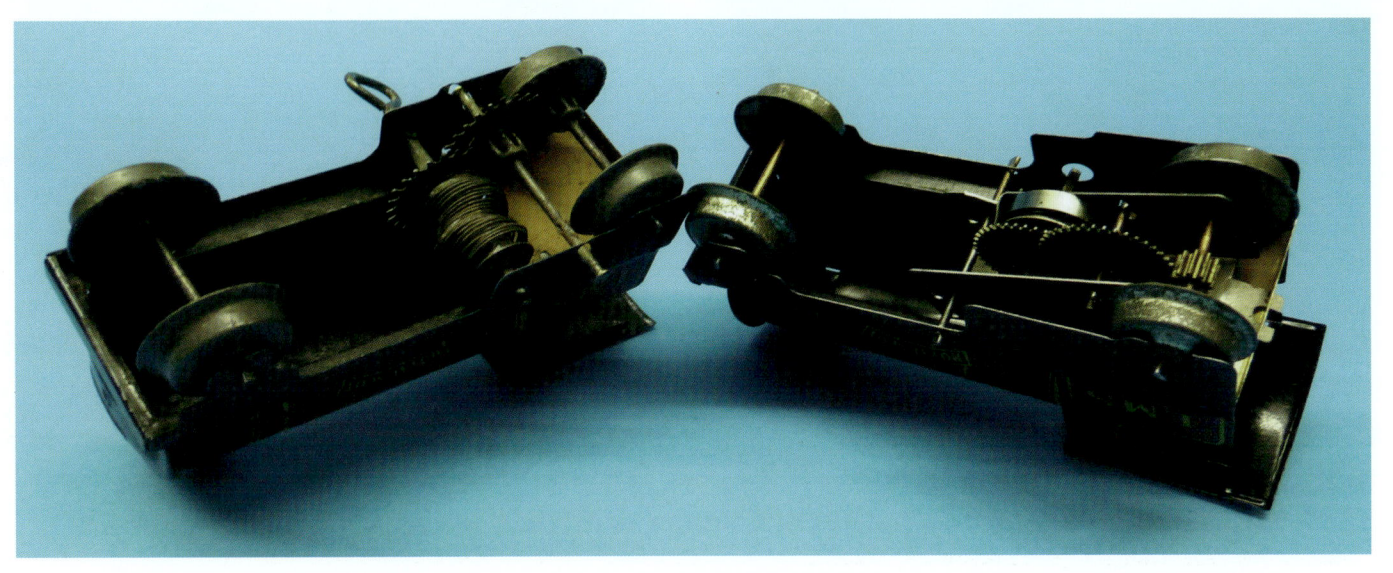

They really were of the "First Quality" as mentioned earlier. Strong, simple, beautifully printed and with immense play value. The sets cost 288/- a dozen = £1.20 each!. The box size on inside measurements 15 ½ inches by 13 inches by 2 inches (394mm x 330mm x 50mm). The April, 1949 Games and Toys had a further advertisement featuring the new wagons, track and accessories such as the wooden signals, turntable etc. One of my sets, No. 10077 has an Inspection Note dated 11th October, 1948 with a note that various accessories will become available during 1949.

The Petrol Tankers No.10075 of 1949

Publicity picture from the 1949 British Industries Fair

Also new in 1949

The 6 inch (150mm) clockwork models to the same scale, featuring:
- 10071 Double Deck Bus
- 10072 Container Lorry
- 10073 Single Deck Bus

They look so attractive alongside the Chad Valley trains.

Set 10077 (Issued 1949-1953)

The wagons were really very attractive. There is the 10074 Model CV Dairies tanker, the 10075 Motor CV Spirit Tanker, the British Railways Container wagon No. 10101 and the Brake Van, No.10076. They all had the simple bent hook and eye couplings. Later issues had black or nickel long link couplings.

67

The four wagons mentioned on the previous page were also available in a boxed set, No. 10090 in 1950. I have two boxed sets, the one with hook and eye couplings also has a single and double Distant wooden signal included in a box measuring 15 inches x 8 ½ inches (381mm x 216mm).

The other has the smaller set with just the four wagons with long link couplings in a box 10 ½ inches x 7 inches (267mm x 178mm), yet I see no different part number.

The container wagons, the British Railways wagon, the milk truck and the cattle truck all had 'Chad Valley' stamped under the chassis – yet no other vehicle. Why?

A busy goods yard scene

I have just totalled up all my Chad Valley coaches and wagons. They come to over one hundred, yet I still cannot find an exact date or model to match the many variations I have. In simplistic terms, the pretty Southern and LMS carriages and matching Green and Red wagons all had the original hook and eye couplings and metal wheels until 1951. I have some Southern Green carriages printed "British Railways" with long black link couplings, metal wheels and crimped axle ends. I also have similar "British Railways" carriages in Red with plastic wheels, crimped axle ends and hook and eye couplings.

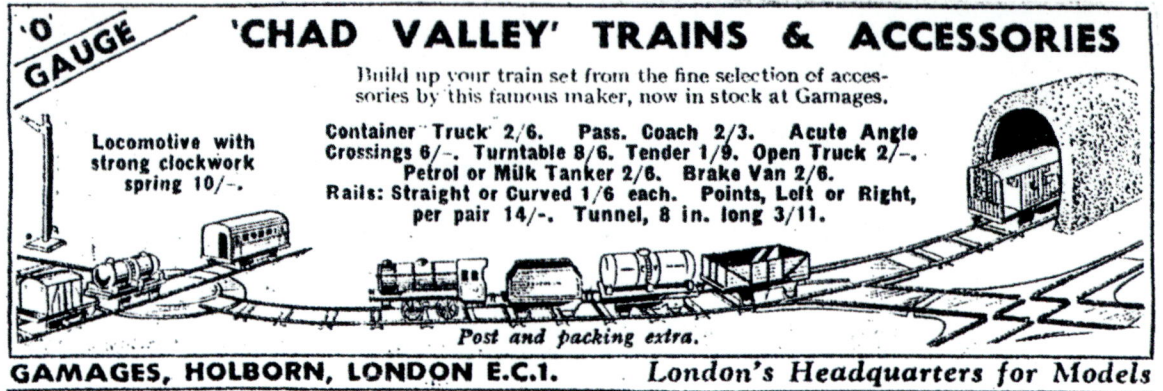

The Gamage's advertisement left, mentions a tunnel, 8 inches long (203mm) at 3/11d (£0.20p). I can find no mention of a tunnel in any of their catalogues. I have three different tunnels of the period, one even 8 inches long, having a handwritten note it is "Chad Valley", but no positive proof.

70

I cannot see either when/why the cream Model CV Dairies tanker was superseded by the light blue 'Fresh Milk' tanker, yet kept the same number – 10074.

Somewhere in the West of England

Set 10223 (1954/1955)

The original 10100 carriages were themselves superseded by the carmine and cream (commonly called 'blood and custard') coaches printed "Master Cutler" in 1951. These had the long link coupling and then the three link couplings. The catalogues record them as No. 10160, but there is an anomaly here. These original No. 10160 coaches all had the long link coupling, but the later series, with the three link chain coupling, all have the number 10129 printed on the side. Me thinks someone has blundered, as this was the number of the metal, circular base junction double signal!

72

The later issue petrol tankers, 10063 "Esso" and 10064 "Regent" all had the long link coupling and two filler domes, yet I also have an "Esso" tanker with a single filler dome.

What I don't understand is why this beautiful train system should have in its seven year life, three distinct, incompatible coupling systems.

The original hook and eye was perfect. The long link type difficult and the final three link chain type well nigh impossible for young fingers – and not so young too! Why?! The systems could not connect!

The Magical Box Cover, 1945 - 1952

The Express rushes by - 1950

1950

1950 was a boom year for Chad Valley trains. They now featured eight sets including a boxed set, No. 10090 with the four new wagons and listing for the first time the individual items previously only available in sets:-

10098 tender, 10099 open goods truck, 10100 passenger coach, now supporting 'British Railways' on the side rather than the original 'Southern' and 'LMS'. Finally, 10102 the engine.

COMPLETE TRAIN SETS, "O" GAUGE.

No.	Description
10111	Engine, Tender, Coach, 8 Rails, (pressed).
10113	,, ,, 2 ,, 8 ,, (pressed).
10114	4 Pieces, Tunnels, etc. 8 ,, (pressed).
10077	4 ,, Passenger Set, 8 ,, (pressed).
10078	6 ,, Goods, 8 ,, (brass).
10079	6 ,, ,, 8 ,, (steel).
10080	6 ,, Passenger, 8 ,, (brass).
10081	7 ,, Goods, 12 ,, (brass).
10116	5 ,, Station Signal Box, 16 Rails (pressed).

All rails in above sets 18" diameter.

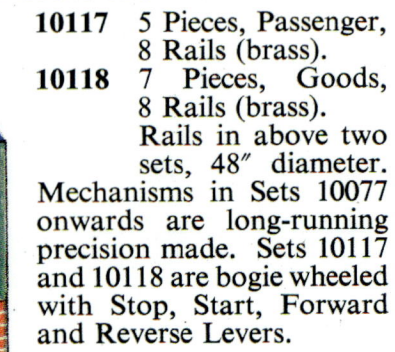

No.	Description
10117	5 Pieces, Passenger, 8 Rails (brass).
10118	7 Pieces, Goods, 8 Rails (brass).

Rails in above two sets, 48" diameter. Mechanisms in Sets 10077 onwards are long-running precision made. Sets 10117 and 10118 are bogie wheeled with Stop, Start, Forward and Reverse Levers.

ACCESSORIES "O" GAUGE.

No.	Description
10090	Boxed Set. Petrol Tanker, Milk Tanker, Railway Container, Brake Van.
10106	Solid Section Rail, STRAIGHT.
10109	Ditto with Brake Lever, STRAIGHT.
10107	Solid Section, 9" Radius, CURVED. Solid Section, 24" radius, CURVED.
10108	Universal Couplings for linking hollow rail to Chad Valley Solid Section.
10085	Double Signal.
10086	Points, 1 each LEFT and RIGHT hand.
10088	Acute Angle Crossing.
10089	Turntable.
10074	Milk Tanker.
10075	Petrol Tanker.
10076	Brake Van.
10101	Railway Container.
10100	Passenger Coach.
10099	Open Goods Truck.
10102	Engine.
10098	Tender.

New vans for 1950

Chad Valley added to the 6 inch clockwork range of vehicles with a 10133 Removal Van and a 10134 Buffet Van, featuring 'Mac's Snacks'. An unusual choice, don't you think?

Everyone needs a break!

77

Reading the small print of this catalogue also shows their new sets, No. 10117 and 10118 featuring the new De Luxe 4-4-0 engine. My set has an inspection certificate dated 1st November, 1950, so only released at the end of the year.

All stations had young train spotters, here collecting the new engine in 1951

1951

British Railways engines and container wagons with the long link couplings from 1951.

Something happened in 1951 which upset the production side of the Chad Valley trains. They now featured twelve sets and an explosion of new products, again listed separately. A brief resume shows:- 10158 Opencast Coal truck, 10159 British Railways truck, 10160 the 'Master Cutler' coach, 10161 the Milk container. An interesting model this, as one side is printed with the door closed, the other side with the door printed open! 10162 is the Cattle truck container, 10163 the Esso Petrol tanker, 10164 the Regent petrol tanker as well as 10125 the Half Signal Box and 10126, the full double sided Signal Box. What surprised me was 10128 the station named 'Bognor Regis'. An unusual selection, but a very popular holiday location for the wealthy businessman before the advent of foreign travel.

Three new accessories introduced in 1951

No. 10125 Half Signal Box (Left)

No. 10126 Full Signal Box (Right)

No. 10128 The 'Bognor Regis' Station (Bottom)

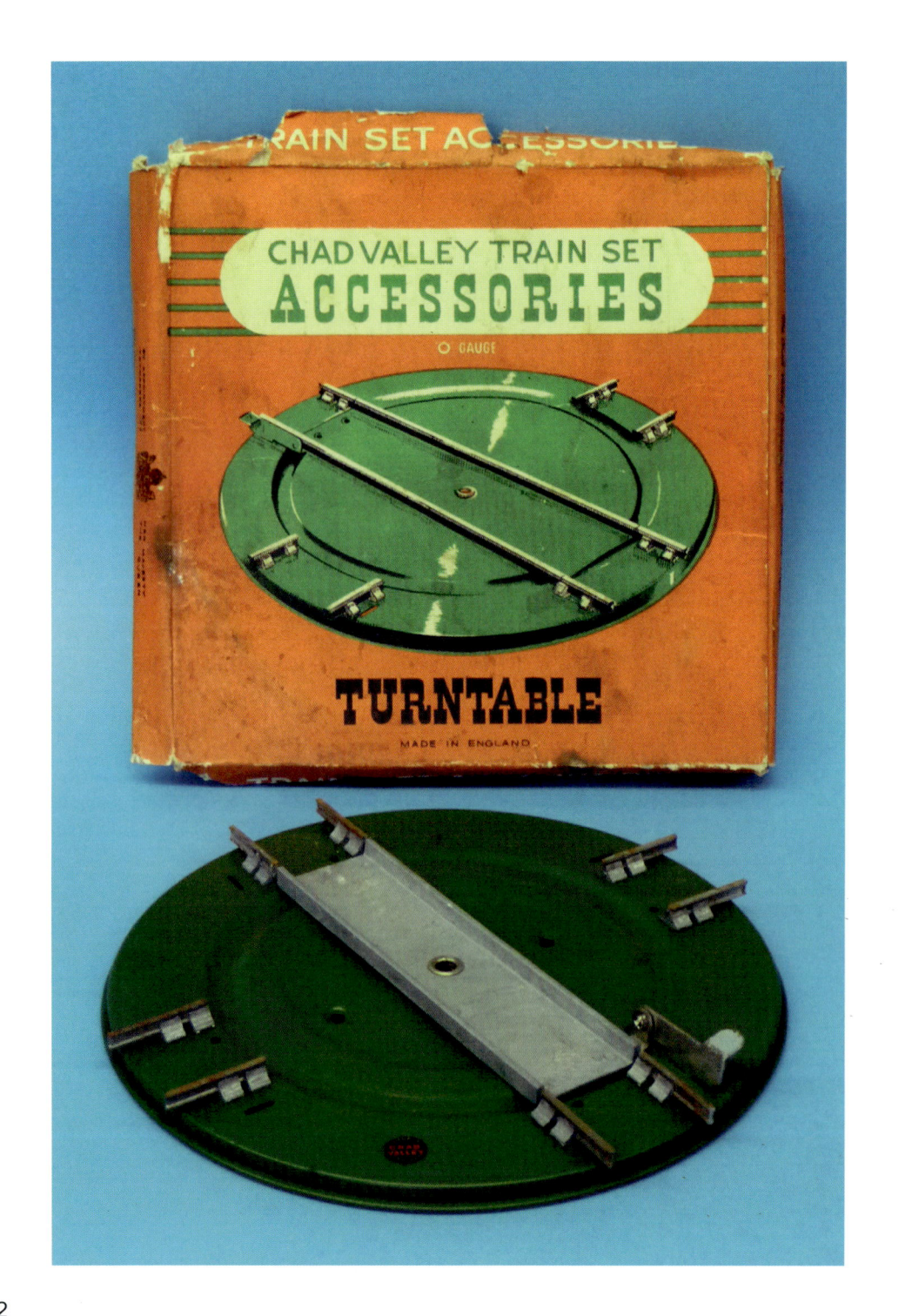

More Chad Valley Accessories

The plain green turntable, No. 10089, left came in an attractive orange box and was made between 1949 and 1954.

The buffers No. 10110 came in a plain brown cardboard box and were available from 1951 to 1954.

An acute angle crossing, No. 10088 was also available.

The left hand 9" radius point, No. 10086 and matching right hand point, No. 10087, above were made between 1949 and 1954.

Boxes of track were also available between 1949 and 1954. The picture right shows a box of a half-dozen straight section track.

The guarantee top right was found in all of the boxed train sets and seems to relate mainly to the quality of the spring mechanism!

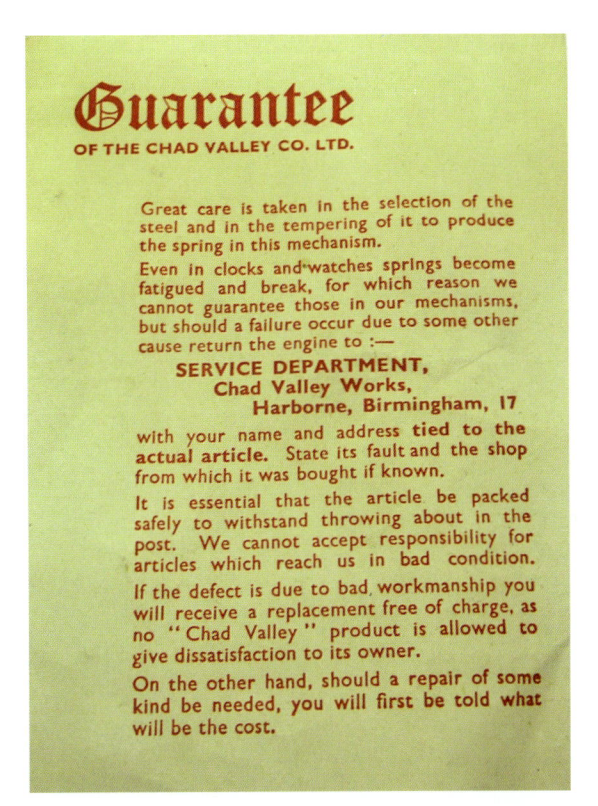

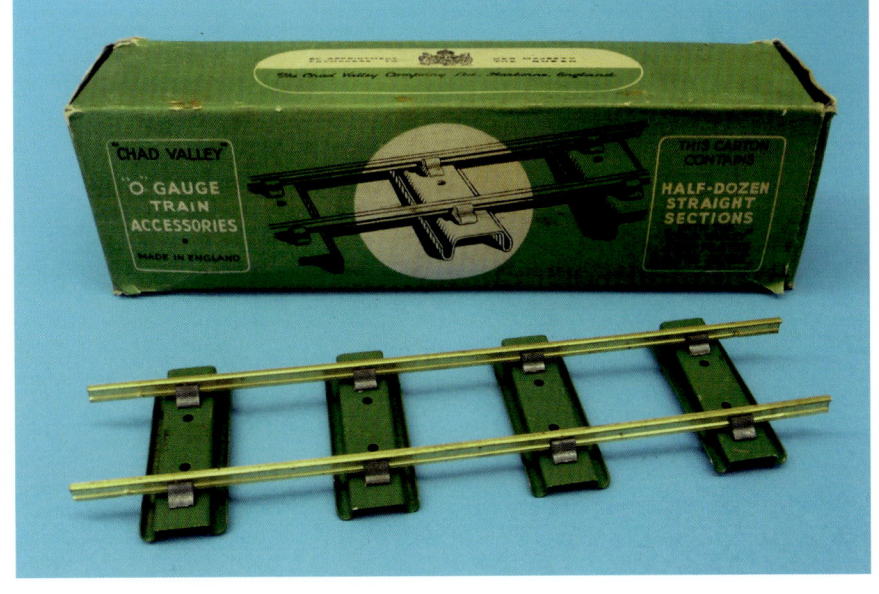

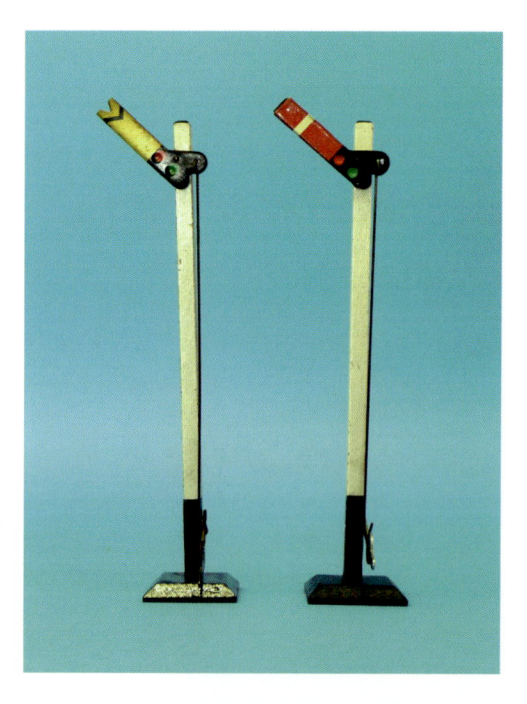

Signals

The single wooden Distant (yellow) signal No. 10084B and the Home (red) signal No. 10084A, far left, and the double wooden junction signals No. 10085B and 10085A, left, were only available between 1949 and 1951.

The metal signals (bottom left) replaced the wooden ones and were available from 1952 to 1954. The single signal was No. 10142 and the double junction signal No. 10129.

In 1951, Chad Valley introduced their beautiful 24 inch radius points No. 10157, but sadly never made a matching acute angle crossing. The points were deleted in 1954.

The distinctive Chad Valley trade mark (bottom right) was found on the base of the wooden signals.

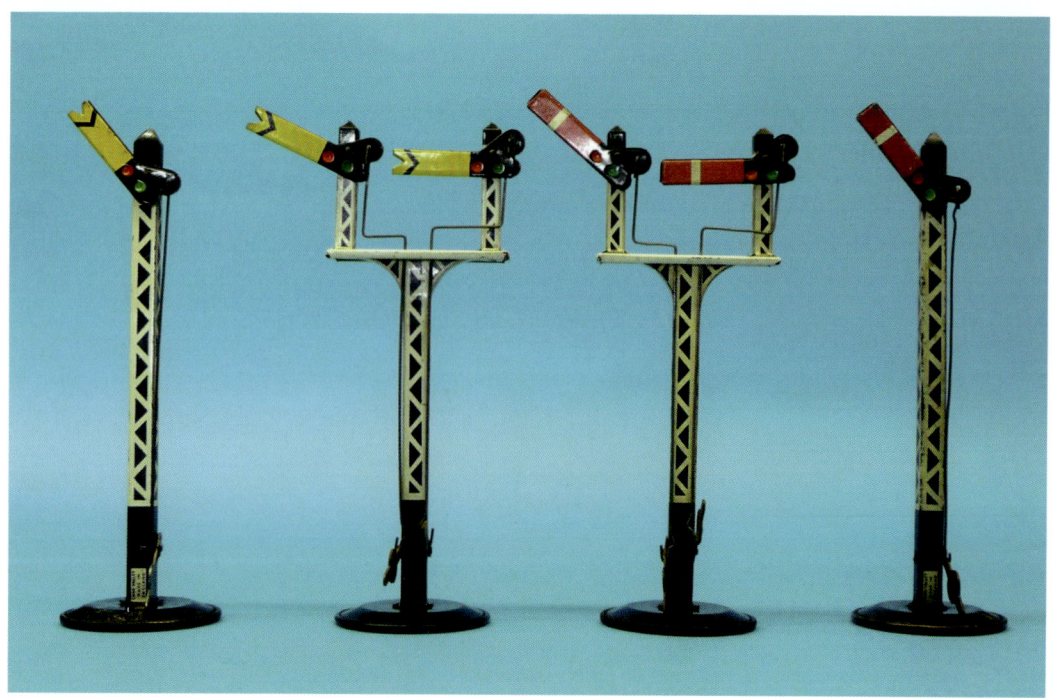

The 10102 Engine

The 10102 engine tree is complicated.

The original engines were beautifully made, with printed cab controls and the set number 10063 on the cab floor. Then there was the same engine but with "British Railways" printed on the tender with a cream lining. These have both the long link and the three link chain coupling. A simpler version which I have not found listed has 3402 and 'British Railways' printed in a brass colour on the cab side, while the tender has 'British Railways' printed in black with a black border. Examination underneath shows a simpler, less expensive mechanism but the interesting feature is the box. The box shows a GWR 'King' Class loco drawing and printed on the end - "This model is primarily intended to run on the carpet, but will run on rails". A carpet train!! I have one with no rear coupling link, or hole for one in the tender. Also one with the original hook and eye coupling. These cheaper engines only had printed hand rails on the boiler, not the wire type.

A peculiar thing is I also have two red CV trucks with the original hook and eye coupling, but a totally different size and base stamping! The original trucks I have are 118mm x 24mm x 41mm high, whereas the two on the lower shelf are 100mm x 20mm x 44mm. When? Where? How? I simply do not know.

The final version of the 3402 engine came out in 1953 with "British Railways" on the tender. No. 10215 had both reversing and brake controls and a totally different 'bent' type connecting rod, not unlike the Hornby type. It had the three link chain couplings even between the loco and tender! (See page 79.)

Midget Train Set

Another new model in 1951 was in the Chad Valley 'Midget' (Mechanical) range when they introduced No. 9556 a miniature train set (above). This is a die cast tank engine body, clockwork! Some 2 ½ inches long (63mm) with an open truck and a coach. (I don't have the coach) A clever little thing, but why produce it? Its range minimal, yet quite expensive, costing 60/- a dozen = 5/- each = £0.25p.

New signals replaced the earlier wooden ones. 10129 is the double arm signal with a metal post and circular metal base, while 10142 is the same single arm signal. They were available for both home and distant signals. (See page 84.)

Instructions for building the track (right) were included with with boxed sets.

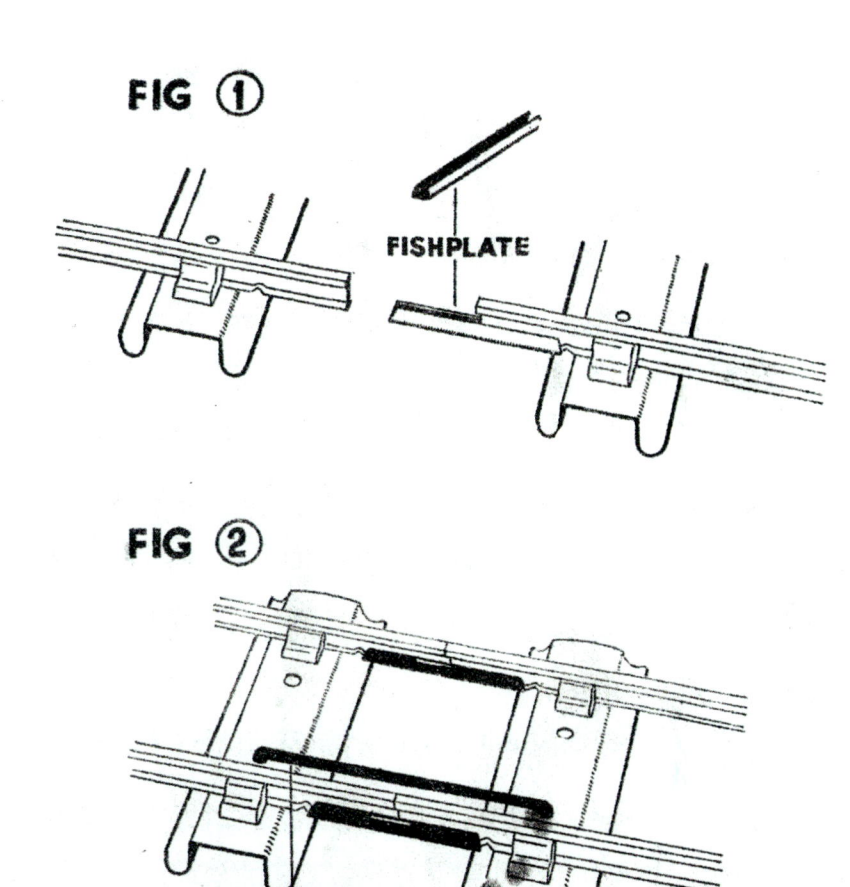

Instructions for Building Track.

In building the Track, the first operation is to fit all the Fish Plates to the lines (see Fig. 1) and push them well up against the stops. Repeat this for each rail section on one end of the rail only.

When all the Rails have been clipped they are then connected together and the connecting links are then inserted into the holes of the sleepers where they join two rail sections (see Fig. 2).

Set 10111 (Issued 1951-1957)

Finally, the longest train set in production was introduced in 1951.

The baby 10111 set, again in British Railways green or red livery with the cab side number 4302.

It lasted up to 1957.

The set comprised an engine, tender and a single coach with an oval of 9 inch (225mm) diameter pressed steel track, much smaller than the usual Chad Valley pressed steel track.

Set 10113

For 1950 only, Chad Valley also produced an identical set to No. 10111 shown on the previous page, but with two coaches.

Like most collectors, I ignored these juvenile sets when collecting Chad Valley trains as too childlike. It took me ages to find them – like hen's teeth! These sets stayed in production right up to the end of the Chad Valley train system in 1957. However, it had a second life, because noted historian, friend and collector of the cheaper international toy trains (he has samples of over 500 different makes) Bryan Pentland found a couple of carriages so identical in shape that they had to come from the same tools. They were marked S.A.R. - South Africa Railways. So, if there were coaches, there must be a locomotive!?

Correspondence followed with Cape Town friends in this international brotherhood of toy train collectors and ended in extraordinary luck. Brian Hodgson of Claremont, Cape Town called on a local toy fair and found an identical loco body and tender to this Chad Valley 4302 – no chassis or wheels, and marked 3132 Class 15F. It is made by Sturdy Products of Durban, S.A. It has an almost orange boiler and cab with a yellow chassis and cab roof.

I had a spare CV clockwork chassis and it fitted perfectly, matching the slots etc. It seems the tools must have been sold on to this South African manufacturer in 1958. A rare beast indeed. All I need now are the cylinders and connecting rods.

De Luxe 4-4-0 engine No. 10138

The 1951 catalogue introduced the 'Pride of the Line', certainly on my layout, with the magnificent De Luxe 4-4-0 engine No. 10138. Everything about it is quality, including the superb clockwork mechanism.

With this engine and tender in BR Express Passenger Blue livery came the famous 'Tube' bogie coaches. No. 10139 Coach De Luxe and No. 10141 Passenger Guards Van De Luxe. No. 10140 was never issued – could it have been a restaurant car? Who knows? Both carried the "Flying Scotsman" printed coach boards. On most of the De Luxe engines I have seen, the key shaft is on the left, facing forwards. However, I have heard of such models with the key shaft on the right, as in the black & white photograph. Perhaps a batch of mechanisms was made such and it was easier to alter the body tooling? A guess?

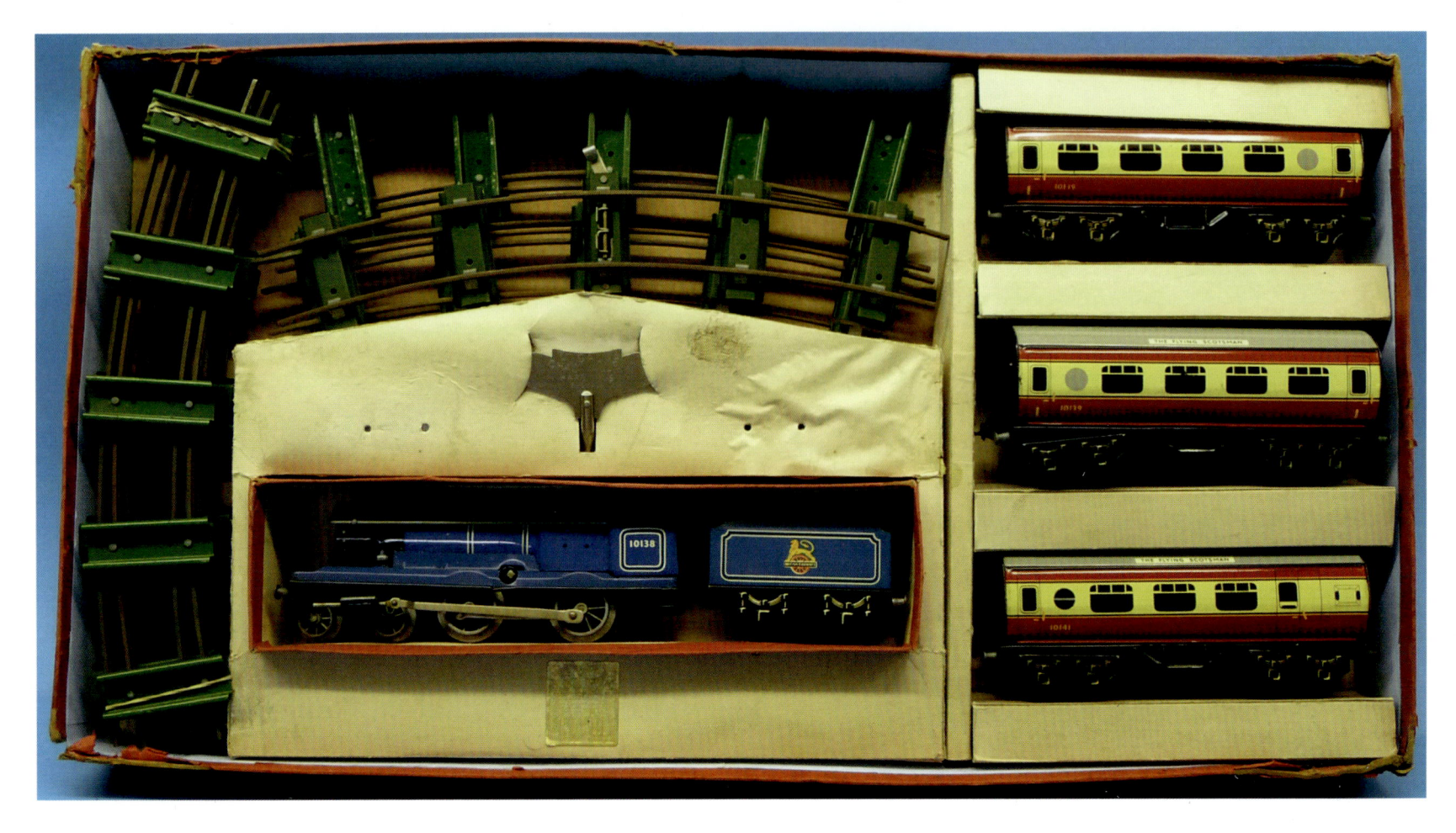

A late 1951 price list refers to this new engine as a 'Lord Nelson' type, though bearing no such resemblance.

This set, comprising the engine, tender, two coaches and a Brake Van had to have new 2ft radius (600mm) track as it would not traverse the original Chad Valley track system. Again, so strong, simple. A real quality product. I played with my set for hours and hours as a boy.

There is also a De Luxe freight set containing the Open Cast Coal wagon, the Cattle container wagon and the Brake van.

In the 1980's, I somehow came across a large store of Chad Valley wagons and coaches in an old airfield warehouse in Norfolk. Amongst the stock was 40 of these 'Tube' carriages in mint condition and scores of wagons. Quite a find!

Doubtless to have a cheaper engine in the range, the 1952 catalogue showed a Black BR Tank engine (i.e. No tender) No. 10210. It had the large early BR emblem on the tank sides, but I have never, ever seen one. I do not think it ever made it into production, though it is quite attractive. I had another good friend, John Brogdale adapt a Chad Valley engine and make a replica for me.

10210

From the 1952 catalogue

The British Railways Coal Wagon

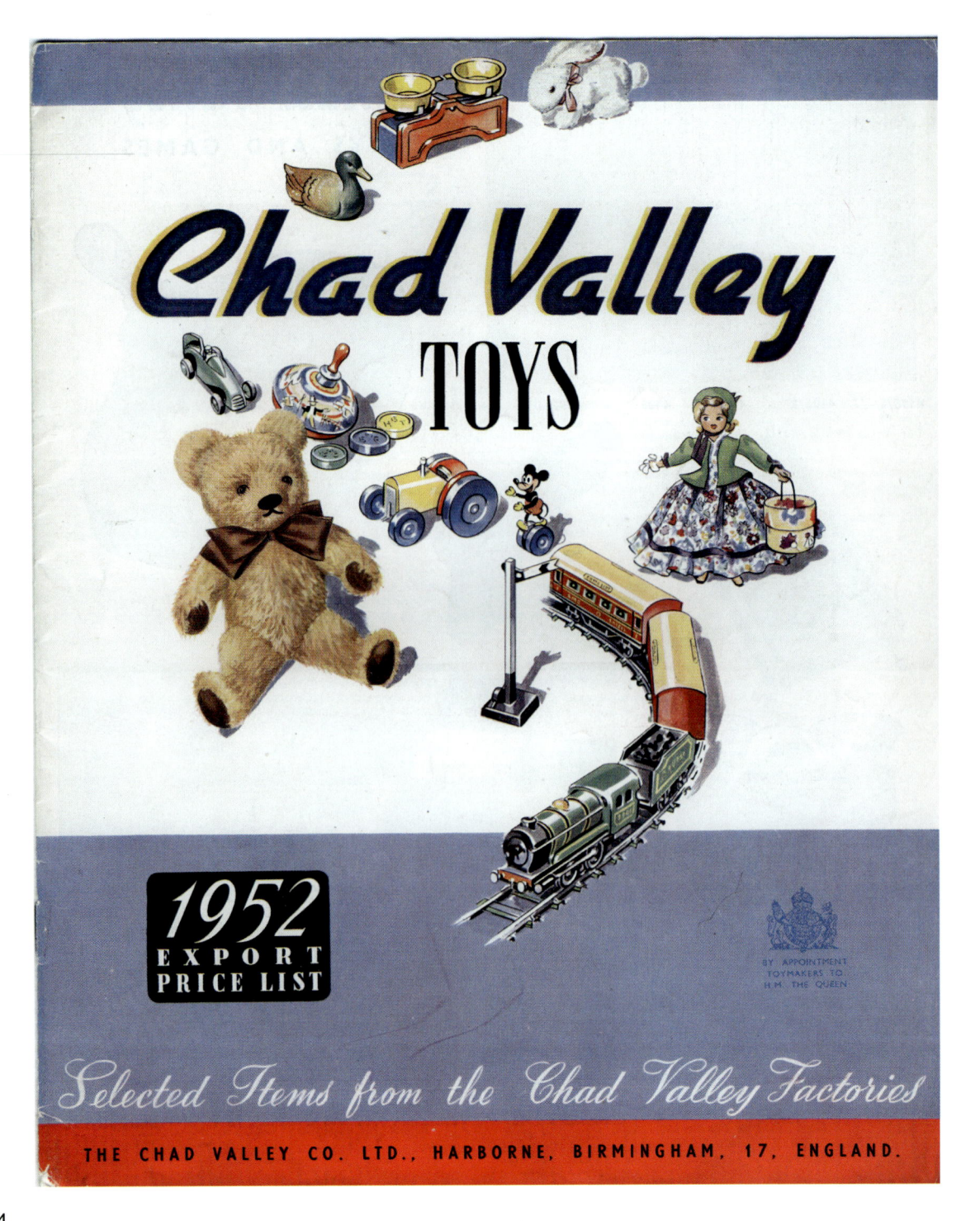

1952 Export Price List

Chad Valley produced new price lists each year and it is interesting to compare the way prices changed. The 1951 and 1952 export price lists printed on the following page show a significant decrease in prices over the two years.

The UK faced a balance of payments crisis in 1952 which might account for the drop in export prices by Chad Valley.

In a memorandum to Cabinet in January 1952, the Chancellor of the Exchequer The Right Hon R.A Butler said:

"We are faced with a substantial balance of payments deficit. Two factors have been responsible. On the import side, prices have risen against us and there have been increases in volume too. On the export side, the general conditions are at present unfavourable and our competitive position in certain industries appears to be deteriorating………We have no hope of getting straight unless we can make our exports plentiful and competitive across the whole range of products, by price and by quality and by delivery date."

Chad Valley Export Price Lists

1951

CHAD VALLEY TOYS AND GAMES

TRAIN SETS

10171	Train Set, Goods	242/– doz.
10172	Train Set, Passenger	262/– ,,
10173	Train Set, Passenger	306/– ,,
10077	Train Set, Goods	358/– ,,
10078	Train Set, Goods	380/– ,,
10079	Train Set, Goods	38/6 each
10080	Train Set, Passenger	38/6 ,,
10116	Train Set, Goods with Station, etc.	46/6 ,,
10081	Train Set, Goods	53/– ,,
10118	Train Set, Goods De-Luxe	78/– ,,
*10117	Train Set, Passenger De Luxe	78/– ,,
*10111	Train Set, Passenger	126/6 doz .

ACCESSORIES "0" GAUGE

10090	Rolling Stock, Set of four pieces	136/– doz.
10106	Solid Section Rail, straight	20/– ,,
10109	Solid Section Rail with Brake Lever	25/6 ,,
10107	Solid Section Rail, Curved 9" radius	20/– ,,
10135	Solid Section Rail, Curved 24" radius	30/6 ,,
10108	Universal Couplings	13/– ,,
10129	Double Signal	39/6 ,,
10086/7	Points, pairs L.H. and R.H., 9" radius	151/– ,,
10088	Acute Angle Crossing	65/6 ,,
10089	Turntable	106/– ,,
10074	Milk Tanker	35/6 ,,
10075	Petrol Tanker	35/6 ,,
10076	Brake Van	35/6 ,,
10101	Railway Container	30/6 ,,
10100	Passenger Coach	30/6 ,,
10099	Open Goods Truck	25/6 ,,
*10125	Half Signal Box	19/– ,,
10126	Full Signal Box	35/6 ,,
10128	Station	58/– ,,
10157	Points, pairs L.H. and R.H., 24" radius	176/– ,,
10110	Buffers	55/6 ,,
10144	Rail, Stamped, Straight Section	7/8 ,,
10145	Rail, Stamped, Curved Section 12" radius	9/– ,,
10098	Rail, Straight, Half Section	13/– ,,
10156	Rail, Curved 24" radius with Brake and Reverse Lever	41/– ,,
10165	Brass Rail with Brake Lever	28/– ,,
10142	Single Signal	23/– ,,
10138	Engine and Tender de Luxe	330/– ,,
10158	Truck, Open Cast Coal	25/6 ,,
10159	Truck, British Railways	25/6 ,,
10161	Container, Milk Truck	30/6 ,,
10162	Container, Cattle Truck	30/6 ,,
10163	Petrol Tanker, " Esso "	35/6 ,,
10164	Petrol Tanker, " Regent "	35/6 ,,
10160	Coach, " The Master Cutler "	30/6 ,,
10139	Coach de Luxe	86/– ,,
10141	Passenger Guard's Van de Luxe	86/– ,,
	Connecting Rods, Fish Plates	5/– gross

METAL DIE-CAST PRECISION MECHANICAL TOYS

*9235	Fordson Major Tractor	320/– doz.

MINIATURE MECHANICALS

*9237	Humber Super Snipe Saloon	66/– doz.
*9236	Hillman Minx Saloon	66/– ,,
9220	Razor Edge Saloon	60/– ,,
9221	Traffic Control Car	60/– ,,
9222	Police Car	60/– ,,
9238	Sunbeam Talbot Saloon	66/– ,,
*9223	Racing Car	66/– ,,
9500	Guy Service Van	71/– ,,
9504	Lyons Icecream Van	71/– doz.
*9225	Open Lorry	71/– ,,
9245	Hart Manure Spreader	66/– ,,
9234	Petrol Tanker	70/– ,,
9227	Timber Wagon	72/– ,,
*9230	Milk Float	72/– ,,
*9228	Cable Layer	72/– ,,
*9229	Breakdown Lorry	72/– ,,
9231	Fire Engine	75/– ,,
*9240	Avenger Single Deck Coach	70/– ,,
9503	Tractor	75/– ,,
9244	Farm Trailer	23/– ,,
*9224	Double Decker Bus	90/– ,,
9232	Tower Repair Wagon	94/– ,,
9239	Dust Cart	90/– ,,
*9242	Commer Hands (Articulated)	94/– ,,
9243	Bulldozer	94/– ,,

MIDGETS (MECHANICAL)

*9550	Saloon Car	31/– doz.
*9551	Single Deck Coach	31/– ,,
9552	Delivery Van (Esso)	31/– ,,
9553	Post Office Van	31/– ,,
*9554	Red Cross Van	31/– ,,
9555	Miniature Loco.	31/– ,,
9556	Miniature Train Set	60/– ,,

PRINTED METAL MECHANICAL TOYS

10005	12" Single Deck Bus	84/– doz.
*10071	Double Deck Bus	59/– ,,
*10072	Railway Container Lorry	59/– ,,
*10073	Single Deck Coach	59/– ,,
*10131	Steam Roller, " To and Fro " movement	40/– ,,
10132	Ladybird	30/– ,,
10130	Royal Mail Van	91/– ,,
*10069	Overhead Railway	152/– ,,
*10046	Remote Control Car	240/– ,,
11060	Bumper Car	30/– ,,
11061	Jumping Kangaroo	40/– ,,
11062	Gambolling Ape	40/– ,,
11063	Jumping Frog	40/– ,,
10133	Removal Van	59/– ,,
10134	Buffet Car	59/– ,,

EDUCATIONAL GLOBES (METAL)

*10174	Terrestrial Globe with Time Disc, 5" diameter, 12.70 cm.	38/– doz.
*10152	Terrestrial Globe, 4½" diameter, 11.45 cm.	33/– ,,
10175	Terrestrial Globe with Time Disc, 4½" diameter, 11.45 cm., in French	35/– ,,

METAL NON-MECHANICAL TOYS

10070	High Flyer Top	8/– doz.
10146W	Small Drum	32/– ,,
10149	8" Drum Sticks (Wood), wrapped ½ doz. pairs	64/– gross pairs
*10008	Scales	30/– doz.
10121	Watering Can	50/– ,,
11059	Spade (All Metal), length 9", 22.90 cm.	70/– gross
10122	4½" Pail, 11.45 cm.	148/– ,,
*10123	6¼" Pail, 15.87 cm.	21/– doz.
*10124	7¼" Pail, 17.80 cm.	30/– ,,
*10169	Circular Pile Ups	56/– ,,
9558	Nursery Clock	152/– ,,

1952

TRAIN SETS "O" GAUGE

*10111	Train Set, Passenger	81/9 doz.
10181	Train Set, Goods (Reversing Engine)	208/– ,,
10182	Train Set, Passenger (Reversing Engine)	208/– ,,
10173	Train Set, Passenger	184/– ,,
10077	Train Set, Goods	197/– ,,
10078	Train Set, Goods	210/– ,,
10079	Train Set, Goods	21/3 each
10080	Train Set, Passenger	21/3 ,,
10116	Train Set, Goods with Station Set	26/– ,,
10081	Train Set, Goods	29/6 ,,
10195	Train Set, Passenger, with track layout and Reversing Engine	35/9 ,,
10118	Train Set, Goods de Luxe No. 2	43/6 ,,
*10117	Train Set, Passenger de Luxe No. 2	43/6 ,,

Size 10111, in display carton, 10½" x 8½" x 2¼"
Sizes 10181/2, in box 13⅝"x13⅜"x2¼"
Sizes 10173/10080 inclusive, in box 18" x 14" x 2"
Sizes 10116 and 10081, in box 21" x 16" x 2½"
Size 10195, in box 25" x 16⅜" x 2¼"
Sizes 10118/10117, in box 23½" x 13" x 2½"

ACCESSORIES "O" GAUGE

*10125	Half Signal Box	10/10 doz.
10126	Full Signal Box	19/9 ,,
10128	Station	32/3 ,,
10142	Single Signal	14/3 ,,
10129	Double Signal	25/6 ,,
10102	Engine and Tender	80/9 ,,
10138	Engine and Tender de Luxe	184/– ,,
10090	Rolling Stock, set of 4 pieces	76/3 ,,
10158	Truck, Open Cast Coal	14/3 ,,
10159	Truck, British Railways	14/3 ,,
10101	Container	17/– ,,
10161	Container, Milk Truck	17/– ,,
10162	Container, Cattle Truck	17/– ,,
10100	Coach	17/– ,,
10160	Coach, " The Master Cutler "	17/– ,,
10074	Tanker, Milk	19/9 ,,
10163	Petrol Tanker, " Esso "	19/9 ,,
10164	Petrol Tanker, " Regent "	19/9 ,,
10076	Brake Van	19/9 ,,
10139	Coach de Luxe	48/– ,,
10141	Passenger, Guards Van de Luxe	48/– ,,
10086/7	Points, pairs L.H. and R.H., 9" radius ... pairs	84/6 ,,
10157	Points, pairs L.H. and R.H., 24" radius ... pairs	98/6 ,,
10088	Crossing, Acute Angle	36/6 ,,
10089	Turntable	59/3 ,,
10110	Buffers	31/– ,,
10145	Rail, Stamped, Curved Section, 12" radius	7/3 ,,
10144	Rail, Stamped, Straight Section	6/– ,,
10098	Rail, Straight, Half Section	7/3 ,,
10106	Rail, Straight, 8" length	11/3 ,,
10109	Rail, Straight with Brake Lever	14/3 ,,
10107	Rail, Curved, 9" radius	11/3 ,,
10135	Rail, Curved, 24" radius	17/– ,,
10156	Rail, Curved, 24" radius with Brake and Reverse Levers	23/– ,,
10165	Rail, Straight with Brake and Reverse Levers, 24"	15/9 ,,
10108	Universal Couplings ...packets	7/3 ,,
10198	Points, pairs (pressed metal) L.H. and R.H., 12" radius... pairs	70/6 ,,
10199	Acute Angle Crossings (pressed metal), 12" radius	31/3 ,,
10196	Set of Pressed Metal Points—pairs, Acute Angle Crossing and 4 Half Section Rails	113/– ,,
10197	Half Length Straight Pressed Rails	4/9 ,,
	Connecting Rods, Fish-plates	3/– gross

METAL DIE-CAST PRECISION MECHANICAL TOYS

*9246	Fordson Major Tractor (new design). Length 7", height 4½" approx., weight 2 lbs. approx.	22/3 each

MINIATURE MECHANICALS (DIE-CAST)

9221	Traffic Control Car, length 4", weight in carton 4 ozs.	33/6 doz.
*9237	Humber Snipe, length 4", weight in carton 4 ozs.	38/6 ,,
*9236	Hillman Minx, length 3½", weight in carton 3½ ozs.	38/6 ,,
9238	Sunbeam Talbot, length 4", weight in carton 4 ozs.	38/6 ,,
9245	Hart Manure Spreader, length 5", weight in carton 3½ ozs.	38/6 ,,
9507	Humber Hawk, length 4", weight in carton 4 ozs.	38/6 ,,
9223	Track Racer, length 5", weight in carton 4½ ozs.	39/– ,,
9500	Guy Van, length 4¼", weight in carton 5 ozs.	41/3 ,,
9225	Open Lorry, length 4½", weight in carton 5½ ozs.	39/– ,,
*9240	Avenger Coach, length 4½", weight in carton 4½ ozs.	41/3 ,,
9227	Timber Wagon, length 4", weight in carton 4½ ozs.	41/3 ,,
9230	Milk Float, length 4½", weight in carton 5 ozs.	41/3 ,,
9504	Lyons Ice Cream Van, length 4¼", weight in carton 5 ozs.	43/6 ,,
*9242	Commer Hands, length 7½", weight in carton 6 ozs.	63/6 ,,
9247	"Stacatruc" Fork Lift Truck, weight in carton 7 ozs.	70/– ,,

MIDGET MECHANICAL TOYS (DIE-CAST)

9555	Miniature Loco, length 2", weight in carton 2 ozs.	17/3 doz.
9556	Miniature Train Set, length 7½", weight in carton 3½ ozs.	33/6 ,,

PRINTED METAL MECHANICAL TOYS each in separate box or carton

10069	Overhead Railway	76/9 doz.
*10046	Remote Control Car	84/6 ,,
*10071	5½" Double Deck Bus	34/6 ,,
*10072	5½" Railway Container Lorry	34/6 ,,
*10073	5½" Single Deck Coach	34/6 ,,
10133	5½" Removal Van	34/6 ,,
10134	5½" Buffet Car	34/6 ,,
10132	Ladybird	24/– ,,
11060	Bumper Car	24/– ,,
11063	Jumping Frog	24/– ,,
11061	Jumping Kangaroo	24/– ,,
11062	Gambolling Ape	30/– ,,

EDUCATIONAL GLOBES (METAL)

10152	4½" Globe (English) 11.45 cms.	22/3 doz.
*12024	4½" Globe (English) 11.45 cms.	21/3 ,,
10175	4½" Globe (French) 11.45 cms.	22/3 ,,
*10174	5" Globe, 12.70 cms.	24/3 ,,
10200	7" Globe, 17.80 cms.	71/3 ,,

Patterns 10175, 10174, 10200 have time discs.

SEASIDE PATTERNS

12000	3¼" Bucket	61/3 gross
12001	3¾" Bucket	78/– ,,
*10122	4½" Bucket	71/3 ,,
*10123	6¼" Bucket	12/3 doz.
*10124	7" Bucket	17/3 ,,
11059	Spade (all metal), length 9"	51/3 gross
12002	Spade, metal blade, wooden handle, length 16½"	10/9 doz.
12003	Spade, ditto, length 19½"	12/3 ,,
12004	Spade, ditto, length 23"	14/6 ,,
12005	Spade, ditto, length 26½"	19/– ,,

A list of Train Sets and Accessories from late 1951 /1952 showing alterations

Complete Train Sets — "O" Gauge

Pattern No.	Type	Description	Price
10172	PASSENGER	~~The least expensive set, including the long-running Loco with connecting rods and which, unladen, should run 60-ft.. Complete with Tender, two Passenger Coaches and oval Rail Track, comprising six curved and two straight sections, printed and stamped~~	20/- INCLUDING TAX
10078	GOODS	The same Loco and Tender, but with two Railway Containers and Solid Section Oval Track on individual sleepers. (Six curved sections and two straight pieces.)	~~35/-~~ 37/6 INCLUDING TAX
10079	GOODS	Same Loco and Tender, and Rails. Rolling Stock comprises Oil Tanker, Milk Tanker, Railway Container and Brake Van, One Double Signal	45/- INCLUDING TAX
10080	PASSENGER	Exactly the same set as 10079, but with four Passenger Coaches instead of the Goods Vehicles.	45/- INCLUDING TAX
10116	COMPOSITE SET	The same Loco and Tender, but a more composite set, comprising two Goods Trucks, Railway Container, Railway Station, Signal Box, Double Signal and sixteen pieces of printed and stamped rail	55/- INCLUDING TAX
10081	GOODS	A very similar set to 10079, but with 6 curved and 6 straight pieces of Solid Brass Section Rail	63/- INCLUDING TAX
10117	PASSENGER	The set of which every boy can be justly proud. Comprises a Loco with driving and bogey wheels, "Lord Nelson" type, fitted with Track operated Brake, forward and reverse movements; Tender; three Coaches (two Passenger, the third being a composite Coach). The Loco, unladen, in this set should run 120-ft. on the "I" solid section rail, with 24" radius curves	84/- INCLUDING TAX
10118	GOODS	The same de luxe Loco, Tender and 48" diameter solid section rails as set No. 10117, together with 5 pieces of Goods Rolling Stock	84/- INCLUDING TAX

All these Sets carry the Guarantee of the Chad Valley Company and are obtainable through all Chad Valley Stockists.

ALL PRICES ARE LIABLE TO REVISION FROM TIME TO TIME.

10195 Passenger Set with track layout & reversing engine:- 75/- inc. Tax.

Accessories

Description	Pattern No.	Price
RAIL: PRINTED AND STAMPED		
Straight, 10½" lengths	10144	~~xxx~~ ea. 1/-
Curves, 12" radius	10145	~~xxxx~~ ea. 1/3
*RAIL: SOLID "I" SECTION		
Straight 8-in. lengths	10106	1/11 ea.
Ditto with brake lever	10109	2/6 ea.
Curves, 9" radius	10107	1/11 ea.
Ditto 24" radius	10135	3/- ea.
Straight 4" lengths (½ section)	10098	1/3 ea.
UNIVERSAL COUPLINGS For linking hollow rail to "Chad Valley" solid "I" section	10108	1/3 Per packet of 1 doz.
FISH PLATES—For connecting solid "I" section rail together	10127	6d. per dozen Plates
SLEEPER COUPLINGS Wire links	10136	6d. per dozen Couplings
*POINTS—Pair, left and right hand, 9" radius	10086/7	~~xxxx~~ pr. 15/-
" " 24" radius	10157	17/6 ~~xx~~ pr.
CROSSING—Acute angle	10088	6/6 ea.
*TURNTABLE	10089	10/6 ea.
BUFFERS—Spring Loaded	10110	5/6 ea.
RAILWAY STATION	10128	5/9 ea.
SIGNAL BOX—Half section	10125	1/11 ea.
Full section	10126	3/6 ea.
*SIGNAL Double "Home or Distant"	10129	~~xxxx~~ ea. 4/6
" Single " "	10142	~~xxx~~ ea. 2/6
*LOCO WITH TENDER as in Sets 10172, 10078, 10079, 10080, 10081, 10116	10102	14/3
10117 (De Luxe Set)	10138	32/6
ROLLING STOCK		
*Milk Tanker	10074	3/6 ea.
Petrol Tankers "Esso" or "Regent"	10163/4	3/6 ea.
*Brake Van	10076	3/6 ea.
*Railway Container	10101	3/- ea.
Opencast Coal Truck	10158	2/6 ea.
*British Railway Truck	10159	2/6 ea.
Cattle Truck	10162	3/- ea.
Milk Truck	10161	3/- ea.
*Passenger Coach	10100	3/- ea.
~~*Goods xxxxxx xxxxx~~	~~xxxxx~~	~~£x xxxxx~~
Passenger Coach, De Luxe	10139	8/6 ea.
Passenger Guards Van, De Luxe	10141	8/6 ea.

The De Luxe Loco. No. 10138 and Coaches Nos. 10139 & 10141 have long wheel bases and will not negotiate sharply curved track or points. They should be run on the 24" radius track and points for maximum efficiency.

* Marked thus indicates the item is illustrated on front page.

Loco No. 10102 should run about 60-ft. UNLADEN. Loco No. 10138 is fitted with Stop, Start, Forward and Reverse Mechanism, and should run about 120-ft. UNLADEN

The press release party December 1952

The Editor of Games and Toys reported he had been invited to a Press Party in December, 1952, held to introduce the electric, battery powered "Merlin" engine. This used the same tender as the De Luxe loco and was based on the famous A4 Class locomotives of the LNER.

The picture on the left shows the engine named "The Master Cutler" and is believed to be the prototype model. Does it still exist, I wonder?

No. 60027 Merlin

It was powered by two U2 batteries. Under test conditions, the loco ran for 7,000ft the first hour, 6,100ft the second hour and 4,900ft the third hour. An impressive performance indeed.

The engine was received with much enthusiasm and the Editor stated Chad Valley are to be congratulated on this new and undoubted winner.

It must have been prompted by the competition as their arch rivals, Mettoy Ltd., had introduced their Safety Electric, battery powered Merchant Navy style engine a year earlier in 1951.

The "Merlin " engine was sold with the 4-wheel 'Master Cutler' coaches which surprised me as I would have thought it looked much better with the bogie 'Tube' coaches (below) issued with the De Luxe loco. Maybe too expensive?

The 10216 'Merlin' set of 1954

1953 obviously featured the 'Merlin' sets No. 10215 to be followed in 1954 with the set 10216. This was an impressive set too, featuring the engine, tender, two coaches, a figure eight track layout using both pressed steel track, crossover and points – and standard tinplate track, stamped Chad Valley! A feature I liked, taken from earlier sets, is the inclusion of the half signal box No. 10125.

100

Box lid from Set 10216

I must admit I do not understand the Chad Valley track system. In such a short lifespan, to have four distinct different types of track seems strange. They started with the pressed steel track from Garnett, Whitely Ltd., through Burnett Co. Ltd. Then their excellent solid rail track system in brass and then steel. I am sure this had something to do with the brass shortages around the time of the Korean War, 1952 period. Finally, to have a conventional tinplate track system. I really do not know!

ACCESSORIES AND ROLLING STOCK
for use with the CHAD VALLEY (Battery Driven)
ELECTRIC LOCO

No.		s.	d.
10213	Loco only, "Merlin" 7½in., for use with two U2 dry batteries	31	0
10215	Ditto, complete with Tender	35	0
10214	Tender only	4	0
10160	Passenger Coach, "Master Cutler"	3	0
10139	Passenger Coach, "Flying Scotsman"	8	6
10141	Passenger-Guard's Coach, "Flying Scotsman"	8	6

N.B.—10139 and 10141 have long wheel bases and fitted with bogies and 8 wheels.

10076	Brake Van	3	6
10161	Milk Container	3	0
10162	Cattle Container	3	0
10074	Milk Tanker	3	6
10163	Petrol Tanker, "Esso"	3	6
10164	Petrol Tanker, "Regent"	3	6
10158	Truck, "Open Cast Coal"	2	6
10159	Truck, "British Railways"	2	6
10125	Half Section Signal Box	1	11
10126	Full Section Signal Box	3	6
10128	Station, size 14½in. x 3in. x 3¼in.	5	9
10142	Signal, Single	2	6
10129	Signal, Double	4	6
10110	Buffers, spring loaded	5	6

RAILS. Pressed Metal, 12in. radius
Printed to represent the permanent way

No.		s.	d.
10144	Straight, 10½in. length	1	0
10197	Straight, Half length		10
10145	Curved (12in. radius), length 11½in.	1	3
10145B	Curved (12in. radius) with Brake Lever	2	0
10198	Points, pair of left- and right-hand (12in. radius)	12	6
10199	Crossings, Acute Angle (12in. radius)	5	6

RAILS. Solid I Section Steel, 24in. radius
Mounted on Sleepers

10106	Straight, 8in.	1	11
10098	Straight, 4in. (Half Length)	1	3
10165	Straight, 8in., with Brake Lever	2	6
10135	Curved (24in. radius), approx. 12½in. long)	2	6
10156	Curved (24in. radius), with Brake Lever	3	0
10157	Points, pair of Left- and Right-hand, 24in. radius	17	6
10088	Crossing, Acute Angle (for 24in. radius)	6	6
10089	Turn-Table	10	6

N.B.—10157, 10088, 10089 are made of steel with die-cast fittings and intended for the highest grade layouts.

10127	Fish Plates, for connecting I Section Rail together (1 doz. in Packet)		6
10136	Sleeper Couplings, Wire Links (1 doz. in Packet)		6

COMPLETE SETS

10212	Comprising Loco and Tender (10215), two "Master Cutler" Coaches, six Curved and two Straight Pressed Metal Rails, all complete in box	52	6
10216	Comprising Loco and Tender (10215), two "Master Cutler" Coaches, Right- and Left-hand Points, Acute Angle Crossing, eight Curved, two Straight, four Half Lengths Straight Rail (pressed metal), one Signal Box, all complete in box	79	6

The 1953 Leaflet issued with the 'Merlin' sets 10212 & 10216

1953 did also include a standard Chad Valley engine, in BR light green colour with 'British Railways' on the tender and an entirely new clockwork mechanism with both reversing and brake features. Why would one want to run such an engine backwards? Seems a little weird, or is it me? This catalogue now lists no fewer than twelve factories producing their wide range of toys to over 8,000 retail outlets all over the world.

TRAIN SETS

CLOCKWORK TRAIN SETS "0" GAUGE

All our clockworks are individually tested before packing, and their performance is guaranteed.

10220 Train Set, Goods
Loco., tender, two trucks, 12" radius rails (eight). Box: 13½" × 13" × 2¼".

10221 Train Set, Passenger
As above, but with two coaches instead of trucks.

10222 Train Set, Goods
Loco, tender, truck, tanker, brake van, half signal box, set of 8 × 12" radius rails. Box: 18½" × 13¼" × 2¼".

10223 Train Set, Passenger
Reversing loco., tender, four coaches, double signal, set of 8 × 12" radius rails. Box: 18½" × 13¼" × 2¼".

10224 Train Set, Goods
Reversing loco., tender, truck, tanker, brake van, double signal, signal box, station, set of 8 × 12" radius rails. Box: 21" × 16¼" × 2½".

10195 Train Set, Passenger
Reversing loco., tender, two coaches, half signal box, pair points, angle crossing, figure "8" track layout, 12" radius. Box: 25½" × 17¼" × 2¼".

10225 Train Set, Passenger
De Luxe loco. and tender, two large coaches, set solid section rails, 12 pieces, 24" radius. Box: 21" × 14½" × 2½".

10111 Train Set, Passenger
(As illustrated.) 9" radius rails. Carton: 10½" × 8½" × 2¼".

Above is an extract from the 1954 catalogue

Sales of their train sets continued through 1954 but by 1955 showed a distinct downturn. Train sets only, no accessories listed. It seems railways were out of favour.

By 1957, when the famous comedian and entertainer Kenneth Horne was managing director, the only set left in the range was the baby 10111 set we have mentioned earlier. The 1958 catalogue had just the metal Distant Junction signal No. 10129 as an accessory to their wooden train set.

Chad Valley trains to me have a unique charm, being so colourful, strong and reliable. The system gave immense 'play value'.

So, readily collectable but limited play value today? Wrong!! I have done a lot of work and promotion of the famous ETS company of Prague, The Czech Republic. They are wonderful engineers and make exquisite metal '0' gauge trains. I have adapted their smallest mechanisms to fit into the bodies not only of the De Luxe 4-4-0 engine and the 'Merlin ' engine, but also the standard 3402 series of engine. So, now I can run these either on standard 3-rail electric track, or even 2-rail track if the rolling stock has plastic wheels, or even on original Chad Valley track, battery operated! A standard 9 volt PP3 battery fitted into a Maplin holder with an on/off switch (part No. L90AN) fits neatly into the tender and can give up to three hours active life! It is so much fun seeing these wonderful old trains having a new lease of life. Of course, these mechanisms can be fitted to not just Chad Valley trains, but to Mettoy, Brimtoy and the like.

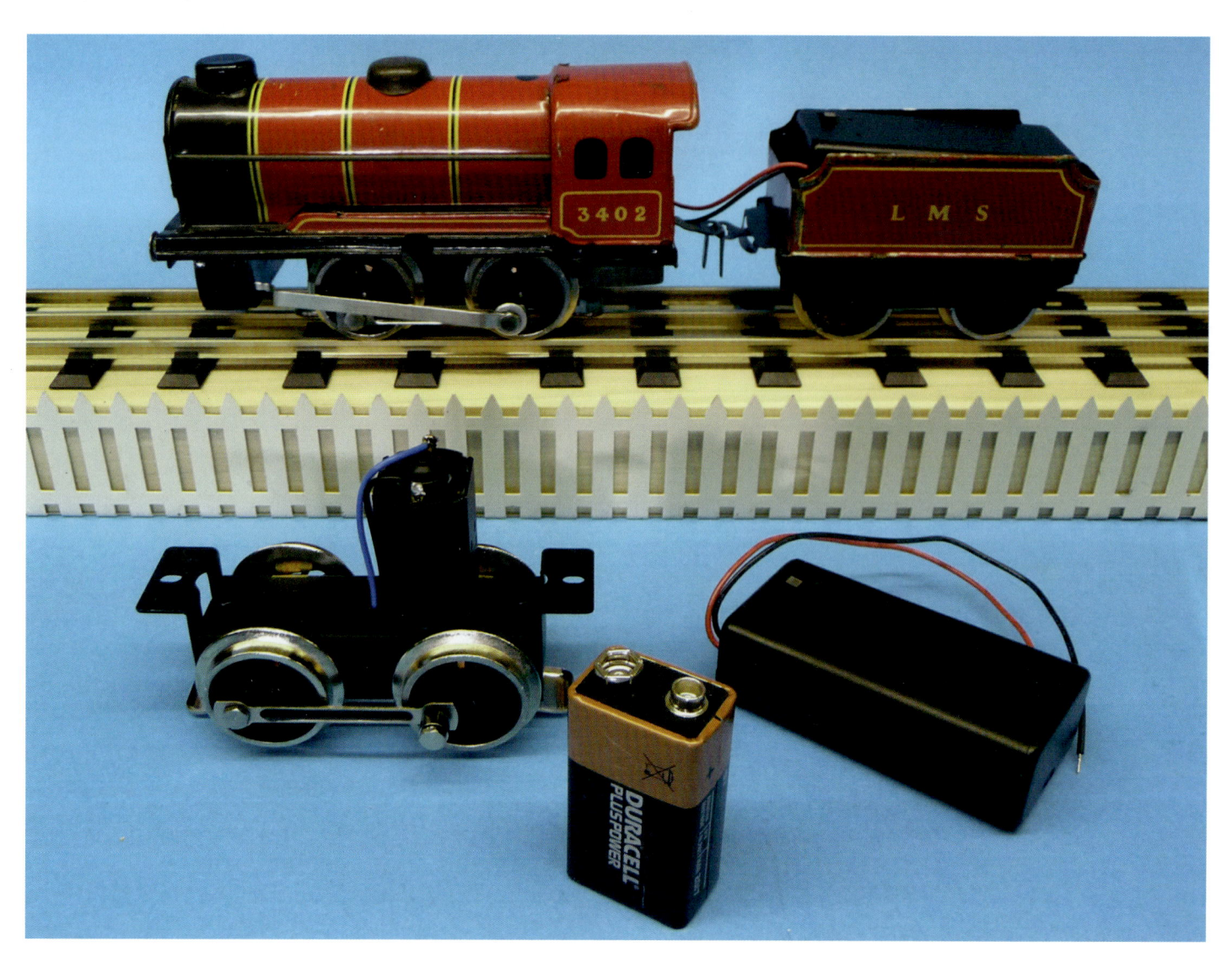

The Chad Valley company moved on, sadly declining over the years. It was sold to Palitoy Ltd., in 1978. It was announced in Toy Trader in July, 1988 that Woolworths had brought the Chad Valley brand name. They too collapsed a few years ago and it is not part of this story. We are only concerned with their wonderful toy trains – and the men and women who produced them for us.

PLAYTIME TRAIN SET 1534

The very last picture of the Chad Valley toy trains, from their 1958 catalogue.

The quality of their toys endures. The Antique Trade Gazette for February, 1985, carried an advertisement from Sothebys featuring the Chad Valley Dennis Delivery Van. It was estimated at £250.00 to £350.00 but sold for £750.00. to much astonishment at the time.

Now you can see and read of the quality of the Chad Valley toy trains. I am sure these too will become collected more seriously. They certainly deserve to be.

You must think that this is the end of Chad Valley toy trains, but you would be wrong. Some years later, I think around 1967 or thereabouts, they made a tinplate, electrically driven Gauge One (G45 track) steam outline engine! No, it is not an April Fool!! They produced a "Melody Train", powered by just one U2, 1.5 volt battery. It ran on a circle of plastic track onto which you set coloured metal sleepers in a particular pattern as listed in the instructions. As the loco ran slowly around, a rotating washer struck the sleeper – and played a tune! Hence, the "Melody Train". Weird, wonderful – a toy in every sense. The engine was made for them in Japan.

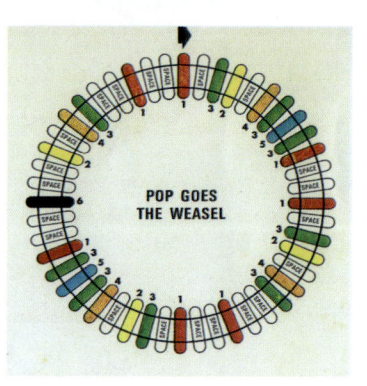

The mystery box set. No idea of contents or when issued? Do you have one?

Extracts from the 1960 Chad Valley Centenary Catalogue

BY APPOINTMENT
TO H.M. QUEEN ELIZABETH
THE QUEEN MOTHER
TOYMAKERS

CHAD VALLEY

CENTENARY

CATALOGUE

CHAD VALLEY
1860 - 1960
CENTENARY

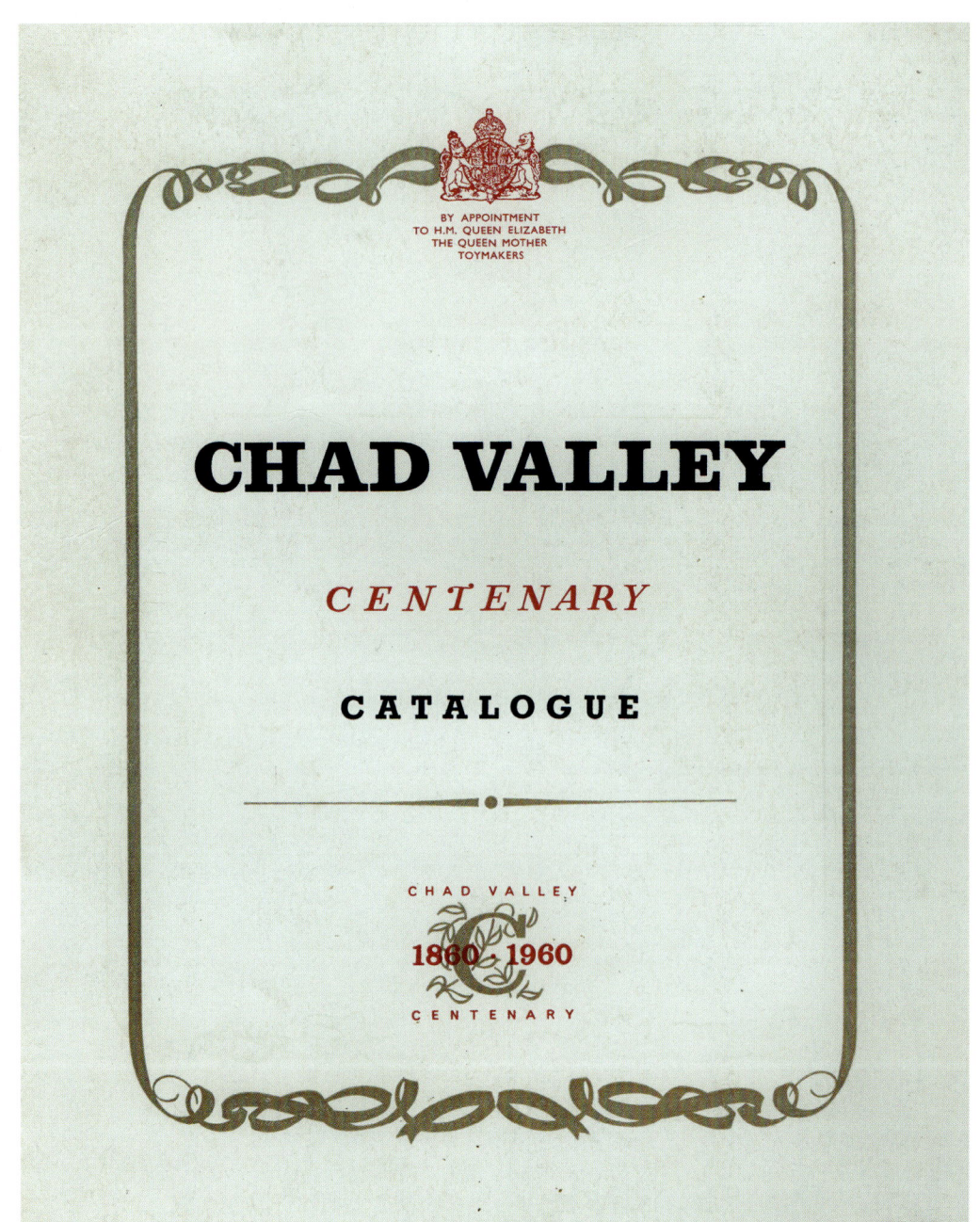

BY APPOINTMENT
TO HER MAJESTY QUEEN ELIZABETH THE QUEEN MOTHER
TOYMAKERS

Centenary Catalogue

The Chad Valley Co. Ltd.

Directors

A. F. HALL, *Chairman and Joint Managing Director.*
R. SWINBURNE JOHNSON M.A., *Vice-Chairman.*
W. A. SILVESTER, *Joint Managing Director.*
W. DESMOND COOKE.
P. W. COLLINSON.

Head Office

Chad Valley Works, Harborne, Birmingham 17.
Telephone : HARborne 3241-6.
Telegrams : Vallchad Harborne.

London Showrooms

9-10 Chandos Street, Cavendish Square, W.1.
Telephone : LANgham 6111-2.
Telegrams : Vallchad Wesdo London.

1960 is the Centenary Year of The Chad Valley Co., Ltd. and its predecessors, Johnson Bros,. Ltd. To mark this occasion the first few pages of our Centenary Catalogue have been devoted to a brief illustrated history of the Company, which we hope will prove of interest to you.

1860 - 1960

SOON after the end of the Napoleonic Wars a printing and bookbinding business was set up in Birmingham by Anthony Bunn Johnson, the son of a soldier who had fought in the wars against France at the end of the eighteenth century and under Wellington in the Peninsular War. Anthony Johnson lived at Handsworth, at that time a small village in Staffordshire, and the works were situated in Lichfield Street, leading out of Birmingham to that town. Under subsequent town planning this road was widened to become one of the principal thoroughfares of the City, now named Corporation Street. The original site of Anthony Bunn Johnson's printing works is now occupied by Maples Furniture Store.

Very little is known about this early forerunner of the Chad Valley Company. One of the original letter headings is in existence, printed in the 1850's and bearing the words: "Established upwards of 30 years." In addition to lithographic printing and book binding the firm engraved printing plates and also manufactured a small range of stationery, including labels and envelopes. The original letter heading is reproduced below.

In 1860, two sons of Anthony Johnson, Joseph and Alfred, set up in a similar business on their own, in premises in George Street, also in Central Birmingham. They traded as Messrs. Johnson Bros., their main products being Stationers' Sundries, including labels and envelopes.

By 1897 Joseph Johnson was running the business himself, assisted by his eldest son Alfred J. Johnson; and in that year father and son moved the Company to a newly-erected factory in the country village of Harborne, at that time outside the city. A little stream, the Chad, flowed nearby, so the new factory was called Chad Valley Works, from which the registered Trade Mark "Chad Valley" is derived. The business traded as Johnson Bros. (Harborne) Ltd., and in addition to Stationers' Sundries, a range of cardboard games was produced.

Below is an early letter heading dated about 1850.

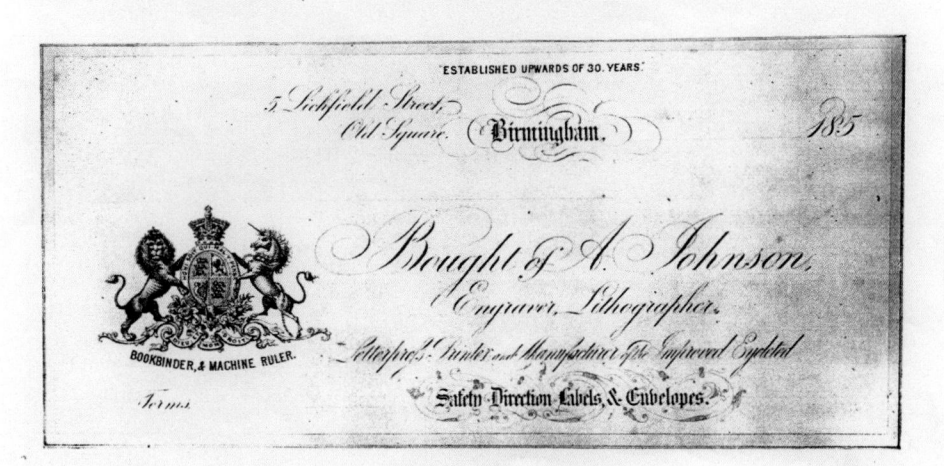

Joseph Johnson, 1842-1904. Founder of the business and Chairman until 1904.

The Clerical Staff at Harborne in 1901.

In 1904 Joseph Johnson died, and his eldest son Alfred J. Johnson, O.B.E., J.P., took his place as Chairman and Managing Director, assisted by E. Dent, who had joined the business in 1887 and steadily worked his way up to be Managing Director when he died in 1946. Also in the Company were two brothers of Alfred Johnson (Arthur and Harry) and his brother-in-law William Riley.

During the years from the turn of the century until the outbreak of the First World War, the Company continued to grow, the range of cardboard games and simple toys being extended from year to year. Children of those days did not enjoy the vast number of types of toys and games that they take for granted at the present time. The games of that period still retained the educational aspect that had been their beginning, and even Snakes and Ladders, was designed to point to virtues and morals.

On the outbreak of the First World War in 1914 all imports of toys and games ceased, which immediately gave a great impetus to the small toy manufacturing trade at home. The range of Chad Valley toys was increased and, in spite of the gradual restrictions in personnel and materials brought about by the War, the business continued to expand. The Company produced its first soft toy patterns—a range of teddy bears—and many other toys were added to the growing Chad Valley catalogue of playthings.

After the end of hostilities more space was needed, and in 1919 the Company acquired the Harborne Village Institute—the foundation stone of which was laid in 1878 by the late Sir Henry Irving. This building was laid out as a printing works, to provide the box covers and labels for the games and other patterns.

(ii)

(iii)

Alfred Johnson, one of the original founders of the business, 1845-1932.

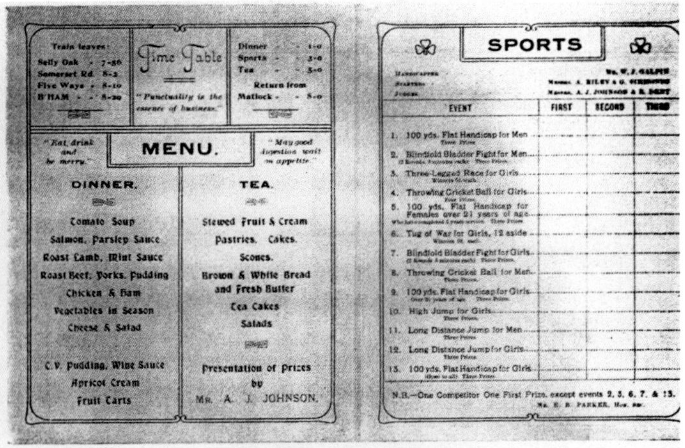

The programme of the Golden Jubilee Picnic at Matlock in 1910.

The soft toy business also needed more space, and the little market town of Wellington, in Shropshire, was chosen as the site of the next factory which began operating as Wrekin Toy Works in 1920. The teddy bear production from Harborne was moved to Wellington, and the soft toy output concentrated in that factory.

At the same time as these new works were brought into production the business was reorganised and the three factories merged into one firm, called The Chad Valley Co. Ltd., which was the beginning of the Company as it is known to-day.

The Directors were:—
    ALFRED J. JOHNSON, O.B.E., J.P., *Chairman and Managing Director.*
    CAPTAIN H. SWINBURNE JOHNSON, *Vice-Chairman.*
    W. A. J. RILEY.
    SIR JAMES CURTIS, K.B.E., D.L., J.P.
    E. DENT.
    F. R. B. WHITEHOUSE, C.B.E.

to be joined a few years later by Mrs. Alfred Johnson and William B. Cooke. E. Dent and F. R. B. Whitehouse then became Joint Managing

The exterior of the Chad Valley Works erected in 1897.

Captain H. Swinburne Johnson, Secretary and later Vice-Chairman, 1879-1947.

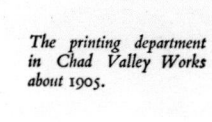

A section of the early box making and games department at Harborne in 1905.

The engineering and tool making shop at the turn of the century.

The printing department in Chad Valley Works about 1905.

(iv)

The final assembly department for soft toys at Wellington in 1920.

The jig-saw cutting shop at Harborne about 1929.

Alfred J. Johnson, O.B.E., J.P., 1873-1936. Chairman 1919-1936.

H.M Queen Elizabeth the Queen Mother being received on the Chad Valley Stand at the 1956 B.I.F. by R. Swinburne Johnson, Vice-Chairman, with Major F. R. B. Whitehouse looking on. H.R.H. Princess Margaret is on the left of the pic

Directors, and A. J. Johnson remained Chairman and Governing Director until his death in 1936, when Sir James Curtis took over the Chairmanship. He was followed as Chairman by F. R. B. Whitehouse, until he retired in 1956, after 48 years with the Company.

During the 1920's the Company very considerably expanded its range of products, and the Wellington factory introduced a range of Fabric Dolls. Then in 1931 the Company acquired the old-established toy manufacturing business of Peacock & Co. Ltd., of London. This Company produced wooden toys, which were also incorporated in the Chad Valley range.

All these developments required more space and a number of big building projects were undertaken. Part of the original Harborne factory was rebuilt and enlarged into a four-storey building—one of the first structures to be built in Birmingham using reinforced concrete and big metal windows. The Wellington factory was also enlarged to give more space for dolls and soft toys. Then in 1928 a new factory was commenced at Harborne, adjoining the main Chad Valley Works. This new building at first consisted of two storeys, to which were added another four in 1932, making the completed building six storeys in all, and a landmark over a wide area of south-west Birmingham.

An important occasion in the history of the Chad Valley Company was the granting in 1938 of the Royal Warrant of Appointment—" Toymakers

(vii)

F. Dent, 1875-1946. Managing Director 1932-1946.

Major F. R. B. Whitehouse, C.B.E., born 1887. Chairman, 1946-1956.

F. C. Hall, 1876-1939. Founder and Chairman of Hall & Lane, 1895-1939.

to Her Majesty the Queen "—an honour which Her Majesty has seen fit to continue to bestow since she became Queen Mother.

During the Second World War the Company's factories switched over to work on Government contracts, and the production of toys was drastically cut. With plants so varied in character, the Company's war-time activities included woodwork, from small instrument cases to ones large enough to contain barrels for anti-aircraft guns; hospital tables to tent poles; electrical work comprising the manufacture of many kinds of coils, electric starters, auto-pilots, etc., children's clothing in the soft toy factory; and charts at the printing works. One factory, by arrangement with the Government, continued in production of certain games and toys, staffed by the Company's oldest employees, a number of whom made jig-saw puzzles for military hospitals, together with draughtsmen, solitaire, chessmen and dominoes for use by the Forces all over the world.

Two of the sons of Alfred J. Johnson were killed in action in 1942—Richard in the R.A.F. and Anthony in the Navy. His eldest son, Roger, the present Vice-Chairman of the Company, served as a Major in the Eighth Army in North Africa and Italy. All three Officers were Mentioned in Despatches, and Lieut.-Commander Anthony Johnson was awarded the D.S.C.

As soon as the War was over the Chad Valley factories quickly changed back again to toys, and the range of products was increased by the addition of metal toys. These necessitated more space and plant, so during the immediate post-war years several metal producing businesses were acquired and incorporated in the Chad Valley organisation.

The first of these extensions was the acquisition of A. S. Cartwright Ltd., manufacturers of aluminium hollow-ware. This Birmingham factory produced a range of tea-sets and cooking sets and other associated patterns.

At the Wellington factory a range of rubber toys was developed, by a process that had been devised just before the War, but only put into full production in 1946. This needed more space, so in that year another factory was found on the outskirts of Wellington (Waterloo Works) and was used for the mass production of rubber toys and dolls.

The year 1950 saw the end of Chad Valley as a private family business, and it was declared a Public Company, with Major Whitehouse, C.B.E. as the first Chairman of the Chad Valley Group. Immediately afterwards, early in 1951, the Group acquired the business of Hall & Lane Ltd., of Birmingham. This Company had been established in 1895 by the late F. C. Hall, whose son, A. F. Hall, is the present Chairman of Chad Valley. The business made tin boxes and allied products, including domestic hardware, and a big range of metal toys; buckets and spades, money boxes, globes and pop-guns. All these patterns and many other metal items were incorporated in the Chad Valley range, which by this time consisted of nearly a thousand different articles.

In 1954 the Company acquired the old-established family business of Roberts Bros. (Gloucester) Ltd., manufacturers of the well-known "Glevum" toys and games. These products were added to the Chad Valley range, and their manufacture transferred to Harborne, where additional space had become available in Wee-Kin Works—a factory on the banks of the Chad, about 200 yards from the main Harborne Works.

Whilst all these expansions of production were taking place the sales staff was steadily built up. The export side was particularly active, and during the years from 1945 onwards the overseas business of the Group expanded very rapidly.

Major Whitehouse retired in 1956, to be followed for two years by Kenneth Horne, who had to resign owing to ill-health. His place was taken by the present Chairman, A. F. Hall, assisted by W. A. Silvester as

(viii)

Harry Corbett with Sooty entertain H.M. The Queen and H.R.H. The Duke of Edinburgh on the occasion of their visit to the Chad Valley Stand at the 1955 B.I.F.

Joint Managing Director. They were associated together in another Birmingham metal toy and tin producing business, The Acme Stopper & Box Co. Ltd., which was incorporated into Chad Valley at the same time—1958.

In addition to Mr. Hall and Mr. Silvester, the present Board consists of Roger Swinburne Johnson, Vice-Chairman, a great grandson of the original Anthony Bunn Johnson, who joined the Company in 1935; W. Desmond Cooke, Sales Director, son of William B. Cooke, a former Sales and Export Director, who started with the Company in 1938; and P. W. Collinson, Director of Administration, who joined Chad Valley after the last War.

The Company now operates seven factories and employs about a thousand people. The present policy is one of consolidation, to be followed by still further expansion, and the Company is now beginning to manufacture and market a range of plastic and vinyl products.

R.S.J.

(ix)

The Chad Valley Directors on the steps of their Headquarters on their Centenary celebrations in 1960.

Front row from left to right:

A.F. Hall Chairman
(Joint MD)

Roger Swinburn Johnson
(Vice Chairman)

W.A. Sylvester
(Joint MD)

W. Desmond Coke
(Sales Director)

P.W. Collinson

Mr Bryan Pentland, Chairman of The Train Collectors Society, holding a Chad Valley locomotive.

Palitoy Train Sets

The Palitoy Train Sets

Gilbert Thomas, in his wonderful book "Paddington to Seagood. The Story of a Model Railway", (published in 1947 by Chapman & Hill Ltd.) wrote about his visit in 1937 to the Model Railway Exhibition held annually at The Central Hall, Westminster:

> "We saw many schoolboys, often accompanied with their by no means uninterested mothers, aunts or sisters, but also men – real men, some nearer seventy than seventeen. It was clear they were drawn from almost every class and calling, doctors and dustmen, solicitors and shop assistants, clerics and cobblers all freely mingling. It was obvious that model railways had succeeded in doing what no other political theory or agitation had yet achieved. It had bridged the social gulf as effectively as it had tunnelled the barriers of age."

To me, one of the parallel joys of this hobby of railways, be they full size or in model form, is the calibre of men it attracts, men of such standing, skill and integrity that they stand head and shoulders above the mass. I have been privileged to meet and know many such men.

The legendary Count Antonio Giansanti Coluzzi of Fulgurex SA, Lausanne who treated me virtually as an adopted son for forty years. We shared a passion for model trains, Rolls – Royce motor cars and life itself. There are others too like Richard Lines of Triang/Hornby Hobbies fame. He gave me such help and advice on my Hornby Dublo book and the V2 project.

The late John Bellwood, chief mechanical engineer at the National Railway Museum was another. He helped me so much on my V2 project too. He once confided to me, in private, that – "You can keep all this scrap here in the Museum. Just give me my V2." But then, he was a Doncaster man! I shared many 'high teas' with the Rev. Edward Beal and his wife, Nellie when on business in Edinburgh. His articles and books from the early 1930's inspired generations of modellers, especially during the long nights of the Second World War. Roger Swinburne Johnson, managing director of Chad Valley was another, as was Arthur Katz, managing Director of Mettoy, but more of him later.

It is not just the older generation either, but men of my generation whose patience, manners, helpfulness, enthusiasm and humour have inspired me. Hugo Marsh, ex. Christies and now a director of SAS Auctions. Barry Potter and his lovely wife, Marie, whose auctioneering skills and toy fair promotions have helped us all. Michael Pritchard, managing director of Peco Ltd., is another. Whenever I have been in contact with that company, I am met with such manners, helpfulness, efficiency from the ladies and gentlemen he employs that it is a joy to deal with them.

It spreads from the top. I have found in my business career that companies echo the character and integrity of the CEO, managing director or the top team. It runs right through the company like the writing in a stick of Blackpool rock.

Such a man was the late Bill Pugh, Chief Design and Development director of Palitoy Ltd. of Leicester. Most of you will not perhaps have heard of him, but almost everyone has used his products. I was in contact with him in the 1980's and had the opportunity to interview him in March, 1982.

The company was founded as Cascelloid Co. Ltd. by Mr. Alfred, Edward Pallet. He was chairman of the British Toy Manufacturers Association in the 1930s. The company was to develop and grow and become part of British Xylonite Ltd., which became B.I.P. - British Industrial Plastics who were to make the famous and fabulous Super Detail range of plastic wagons and locos for the Hornby Dublo range of Meccano Ltd., in the late 1950s.

They called their toy making division Palitoy (Pallet's Toys?) and it was registered in 1935. In 1938, from their Cascelloid Ltd., factory in Abbey Lane, Leicester, they produced the first ever plastic injection moulded toys, vehicles and aircraft. They were made by their chief engineer, Mr. Bramley. The vehicles all had to have a taper design to facilitate releasing the model from the mould.

They made the very first available electric train set after the Second World War finished. Mr. Pugh in his letter stated they were launched at the BIF – British Industries Fair at Olympia, London in May 1949. However, I believe it was May, 1950 from their advertisement in Games and Toys, followed up by a further advertisement in the August, 1950 issue, no doubt to catch the Christmas trade orders. It was an astonishing success, selling £66,000.00 worth in the first two weeks!

It was the first model with moulded rivet detail. Based loosely on the A3 "Flying Scotsman" engine, it was actually called the "Flying Scot". The set comprised an engine, tender, two carriages and ten feet (3 metres) of brass 2-rail track, powered by four U2 1.5 volt batteries. Surprisingly, they chose an 'S' gauge type track, one inch (25mm) gauge. This was new to us in the UK but well known and accepted in the USA for many years. The electric set was No. 9500. However, a catalogue picture shows a clockwork version too, No. 12040 which I have never seen. The innovation was ground breaking, as one would expect from Mr. Pugh. Not only was it the first 2-rail electric system, with roller brass pick ups (copied by Rovex/Triang in their early "00" Princess loco) but it had traction rubber tyres on the rear driving wheels. It had a headlamp moulded unit on the top of the smoke box, doubtless deleted by cost on the production models.

118

It had a large rigid pendulum under the couplings, doubtless to be raised by a ramp in the rail to uncouple. They had needle axles on the loco bogie wheels and coaches which was another first. Much lower resistance than the normal Hornby and Bassett Lowke axles.

The motor was an 'Ever Ready' design, which they supplied as a boost to sell more batteries. I have two versions, identical but with moulded different cab side number – 5006 and 5102. Why go to the expense of such, to me, meaningless alterations. The four wheel, though moulded bogie carriages were in 'carmine and cream' and a peculiar Southern Region moulded green. I have heard of other coaches too in an odd yellow colour (Teak?) and a bright blue, but have never seen them. They had 'British Railways' moulded to the side. They had cellophane strips in the carriage windows and, the only time I have ever seen it – steps moulded under the carriage doors!

Instructions for Operation of PALITOY ELECTRIC TRAIN SET

The Palitoy Train Set consists of a locomotive, tender and two coaches complete with 10 feet of track and a control box in which are placed four U.2 Ever Ready dry cells to supply 6 volts to the miniature electric motor which drives the locomotive. **Because this train set operates on 6 volts it is entirely safe and shockproof.** The miniature electric motor is designed to work from direct current and is therefore not suitable for use on electric light mains without the installation of special rectifying equipment.

1.—ASSEMBLING THE TRACK. Each section of track, of which there are ten (2 straight and 8 curved), is fitted with connectors at one end which enable each section to be connected to the next section. The joints between each section should be pushed tightly together to ensure perfect contact.

2.—FITTING BATTERIES INTO CONTROL BOX. Remove the lid of the control box by unscrewing the centre nut, and place the four U.2 Ever Ready batteries in position as indicated by the markings on the control box lid, two in the upright position and two in the inverted position. Replace the lid carefully, making sure the control lever is located in the slotted side of the box. Then secure the lid by screwing down the brass nut until it is finger tight—do not use force.

3.—CONNECTING CONTROL BOX TO TRACK. It will be seen that a flexible lead terminating in a plastic connector is attached to the control box, and it is this plastic connector which should be connected to the track. To do this pull two sections of the track apart and slide the plastic connector on to one section of track in exactly the same manner as one of the sleepers already on the track. Then connect the two sections of track together again.

4.—TESTING THE TRACK WITH LOCOMOTIVE ONLY. First of all make certain that the control lever on the control box is in the OFF position (CENTRE POSITION). Place the locomotive carefully on the track, then gently move the control lever to left or right; the locomotive will then run round the track. By gently moving the control lever over to the opposite side the locomotive will reverse and run in the opposite direction. If the locomotive is running smoothly round the track the tender and coaches should then be coupled together to form the train. (For hints on maintenance of locomotive, see notes below).

5.—MAKING UP THE TRAIN. The coaches and tender should always be coupled and decoupled on the straight portions of the track. Place the tender on the rails with the coupling hook pointing towards the rear of the locomotive. A slight push of the coupling hook against the coupling bar on the back of the locomotive is sufficient to couple the tender to the locomotive. The coaches may then be coupled to the tender and to each other in exactly the same manner. The train is now ready for operation and can be moved backwards and forwards by movement of the lever on the control box.

6.—AUTOMATIC DECOUPLING AND SHUNTING. It will be seen that one straight section of track is fitted with a decoupling device. When the decoupling bar is pushed into the centre of the track the coaches are detached when passing over this point. By using the decoupler at the right time one or two coaches can be detached at will. Coaches can be automatically re-coupled by reversing the locomotive and shunting the coaches together. Shunting should always be carried out on a straight portion of the track, the locomotive being shunted gently up to the train.

7.—MAINTAINING THE LOCOMOTIVE. In order to the best results from the PALITOY TRAIN SET it is most essential to ensure the maintenance of the locomotive which is really the heart of the train set.

8.—OILING THE LOCOMOTIVE. In order to ensure the long life of the electric motor and smooth running over long periods, **it is absolutely essential to lubricate the motor bearings at regular intervals.** An oiling hole will be found at the top of the locomotive about 1¼" forward of the driver's cab. After 15 minutes' running 1 small drop of any thin machine oil should be dropped from the end of a needle into this hole. A larger quantity of oil will do harm to the electric motor. Remember one drop is quite sufficient. Another single drop of oil from a needle (not from an oil can) should be placed beneath the small pinion on the other end of the motor spindle.

9.—ADJUSTING AND CLEANING OF THE ROLLER CONTACTS. The locomotive picks up electric current from the rails through the roller contacts which are mounted on two springs, on either side of the locomotive on the underside. It will be noted that after a period of running a black deposit will form on these rollers. This must be carefully removed with the glasspaper provided. When cleaning these rollers the springs may be moved out of adjustment. The correct adjustment of these springs is so that the rollers are level with the flanges of the wheels and just touching the rails when the locomotive is placed on the track. If the springs press too heavily on the rails the locomotive will tend to lift off the track at the curves. A very light pressure is all that is required to ensure good electrical contact.

10.—KEEPING THE TRACK CLEAN. Dirt will not permit the flow of electric current. Therefore the track must be kept absolutely free from dirt and grease at all times. **The track should be regularly cleaned with the glasspaper provided if the train is to run smoothly.**

SOME RUNNING HINTS

Remember to lubricate the motor bearings in the locomotive, with a small drop of oil at regular intervals.

On no account should an oil can be used for oiling, the oil should be applied on the end of a darning needle.

Always keep the track and roller contacts clean.

Always remember to remove batteries from the control box after use.

Do not interfere with the working parts.

Do not place metal articles across the track as this runs down the batteries.

Never push the train along the ground as this will damage the drive mechanism.

EXTRA TRACK AND ROLLING STOCK for the PALITOY TRAIN SET can be obtained from Palitoy Stockists in all parts of the country. If you are unable to obtain these from your local toy dealer or store, write to the makers:—

CASCELLOID LIMITED, ABBEY LANE, LEICESTER

Instructions from the lid of the Palitoty Electric Train Set

The 'Flying Scot' locomotive with the carmine and cream coaches, The coaches for this set were similar to those used with the prairie tank set but had a black roof.

The modelling of the locomotive is quite basic compared to the later prairie tank model on page 123. The brass strip across the top of the cab was a crude way of holding the split body moulding together!

CLEAR TRACKS!
FOR THIS POWERFUL *NEW* Palitoy ELECTRIC TRAIN SET

Make room in your windows, on your counter and shelves—for the finest 'value for money' Electric Train Set you have ever sold! A masterpiece of model engineering—perfect in every detail. Powerful electric motor with worm-gearing with complete connecting-rod drive. Remote control Starting, Stopping, Reversing and De-coupling. Entirely shockproof, the set comprises 2—6—2 Prairie Tank Locomotive, Two Pullman Coaches, Control Box and 10 feet of track comprising curved and straight sections—all enclosed in a stout Colourful Display Box which sets the signals for big Sales Success!

Engine driven by Four Standard U2 Batteries, in control box, but can be connected through a transformer to mains.

See this wonderful new model at B.I.F. OLYMPIA
Stand No. N 102

CASCELLOID LTD.
London Showrooms:

An advert from Games and Toys magazine April 1951

A year later, in April, 1951, a new engine appeared – a GWR/BR 2-6-2 Prairie Tank engine. This was an astonishing piece of work, beautifully detailed with all rivets etc., but this time a true 2-rail, electrical pick up through both sides on metal cast driving wheels, on a central strong plastic axle to give insulation.

Bill told me he thought a tank engine would be cheaper than a tender engine. He even produced prototype freight wagons, but was not allowed the finance to put them into production. The box lid mentions a flat wagon, closed vans and a tank wagon. No points were ever made, though their catalogue did show a right angle crossing. No signals or other accessories, it remained simply a toy train. The train sets remained in the company catalogues up to 1959.

The Safety Electric Train Set

The Palitoy Prairie Tank set with the grey roof version of the carmine and cream coaches.

It was powered by 4 No. U2 type 1.5 volt batteries which fitted inside the blue controller.

124

A brief history of the company was written in 1984 when the then owners, General Mills, decided to sell off or close down their English and American toy firms which gives you the complicated ancestry of this once famous company.

It was only on his passing, in June, 1994, did I fully understand the astonishing creative genius of Mr. Bill Pugh. He was responsible for Action Man, voted Toy of the Year in 1966. It was he who invented the Jif lemon juice squeezer, selling seven million a year and tomato shape sauce squeezer, the Domestos bottle and countless others. The plastic ducts carrying hot or cold air to your dashboard were originally designed by Bill for Rolls Royce Motors. Up till then, such ducting was in sheet metal! Certainly he was a man of genius and a privilege to know.

Daily Mail, Friday, July 1, 1994

FOR BOYS, HOW ONE DESIGNER MOULDED OUR MODERN WORLD

Lemon aid: Bill Pugh with his Jif juice squeezer — seven million are still sold annually in Britain

Classic creations: Action Man (above) and ketchup container (below)

In 1965, he decided to concentrate on plastic toys and became director of design, research and development at Palitoy. Heading a team of 22 designers, engineers and chemists, he helped produce a range of electric trains — and Action Man.

The jointed male doll was a massive hit and, in its heyday, almost every boy in Britain had one. Action Man came in a variety of guises — including soldier, polar explorer and deep sea-diver — with an array of ancillary equipment, most of it moulded plastic.

In 1966, it was voted Toy of the Year. But nine years ago, the pint-sized hero lost his long drawn-out battle against the onslaught of high-tech computer games and disappeared from the toy shops.

He was down, but not out — and last year made a comeback as fathers who remembered him from boyhood introduced their own children to him.

Collectors now pay up to £300 for a boxed original.

Mr Pugh, who filled his home in Leicester with his paintings and sculpture, loved to astonish people by telling then he did not even own an Action Man. But at the toy's relaunch, he said: 'Its appeal is timeless. It is a human figure and that is the most important thing there is in a child's imagination. It can be their father or one of their heroes.'

The Astra Railway Wagons

A very popular toy in the late 1930's and immediate post Second World War was the die cast range of guns and searchlights under the 'Astra' name. They were sold by H.A.Moore and Co. Ltd., of 415 Bridgewater Square, Barbican, London. But made by Astra Pharos Ltd., of Landor Works, Askew Road, Shepherds Bush, London. They were well made, well engineered and very realistic models. You rarely see them at Toy Fairs anymore. So, you may well ask, what on earth has this to do with '0' gauge model railways?

A chance find in the Meccano archives when researching my Hornby Dublo book was a photocopy of Astra's 1939 illustrated price list. There, item 11 is a searchlight mounted on a 4-wheel wagon. The caption reads – "A high grade truck and powerful searchlight, very strongly made in die cast metal and aluminium, complete with switch and battery." – all for 4/11 (=£0.25p!)

Item 20 is a gun mounted on a similar truck base. To quote – "A high grade cap firing gun which shoots projectiles up to 20 yards (18.28 metres). Quick loading, ideal for forts and toy soldiers." The price the same – 4/11 (£0.25p) complete with twelve projectiles.

I have one in a khaki green colour and another in a dark/light green camouflage livery. Despite no makers badge, I was quickly able to identify them on a Toy Fair table. I said at the beginning they were well engineered. Stripping them down to clean matted oil and dirt from 70 years use. I was surprised to see they had needle, pin point axle ends. A first in my experience. Someone knew what they were doing.

127

Die Casting Machine Tools Ltd.
Featuring:- Harry Hayseed, The Tricky Track Man

One of my favourite train toys!

I came across the advertisement on this page in the January 1950 issue of Games and Toys. It is brilliant, quite whimsical, so seeing one for sale at a Toy Fair, I pounced on it.

I have a plan to mount two magnets, positive to positive on the couplings so that as the locomotive comes gently towards it – the trolley is pushed away by magnetic force. No actual physical attachment at all. The faster you make the loco go, the faster poor Harry has to pump his trolley.

It leaves me helpless!!

Die Casting Machine Tools Ltd. (DCMT) made a range of diecast toys from their factory at River Works, 152 Green Lanes, Palmers Green. London N13, but this is the only 'O' gauge toy I know.

January, 1950   **GAMES & TOYS**   185

String along with Harry!

Harry Hayseed on the High Wire

Harry Hayseed the Tricky Track Man

The wise toy dealer knows how popular has become the D.C.M.T. sensation of the year —"HARRY HAYSEED." And now, following on the success of Harry on his "Tricky Tractor" comes Harry "On the High Wire" and as the "Tricky Track Man" on his platelayer's trolley that fits all 'O' gauge tracks. Stock and display "Harry" and all D.C.M.T. 'Slikka' Playthings for slicker sales. Write now for full information.

The JUNIOR MECHANIC'S TOOL KIT
for the kids who like to tinker

A real working tool set comprising of screwdriver, hammer, pliers and adjustable spanner all in a workmanlike fitted folding case with carrying handle.

They're DCMT Slikka Toys

DIE CASTING MACHINE TOOLS LTD.

River Works, 152 Green Lanes, London, N.13, England; Tel.: PALmers Green 2271; Grams: Diemechs, Wood, London; Cables: Diemechs, London, England; and at New York, N.Y., and Los Angeles, Calif., U.S.A.

Coming soon!

British Toy Trains

Featuring all those other British toy train manufacturers

Book 2 of 4 - Betal   Mettoy Co. Ltd.   A. Wells Co. Ltd.

For more information contact Michael Foster: mdfoster@hotmail.co.uk
Tel: 07979 241406

Vectis AUCTIONS LTD
COLLECTABLE TOY SPECIALISTS

The World's Premier Train Auction House

Regular Monthly Sales of Vintage & Modern issues, auctioning a variety of gauges from N Gauge to 5" Gauge

Vintage Sales: Late Victorian to 1960's
Chad Valley, Brimtoy, Bassett-Lowke, Hornby O Gauge & Dublo plus Marklin

Modern sales: 1970's to Present day
Hornby Railways, Lima, Mainline, Bachmann, Marklin HO Gauge, Fleischmann, Brawa & Roco

- Free Valuations
- World Record Prices achieved
- All Auctions held on-line reaching a worldwide audience
- Knowledgeable staff covering a diverse range of toys
- Professional, reliable & friendly service

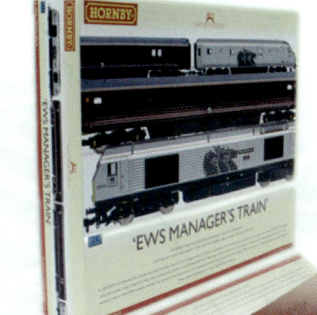

WWW.VECTIS.CO.UK

For more information regarding forthcoming sales visit the vectis website. All Vectis sales are Room Auctions, however, live internet bidding is available at www.vectis.co.uk (except Rugby sales) & www.invaluable.com

VECTIS AUCTIONS, FLECK WAY, THORNABY, STOCKTON-ON-TEES, TS17 9JZ

Telephone - 01642 750616 Fax - 01642 769478 e-mail - admin@vectis.co.uk

Contact Mike Delaney at our Oxford office on 01993 709424

SAS
Est. 1991

specialauctionservices.com

British Toy Trains at Special Auction Services

We auction toy and model trains in all gauges by many different British makers in at least nine sales a year, rounded off by our special Trains Galore sale in December. Every year the sale includes over 1200 lots of commercial models from the large makers such as Hornby and Bassett-Lowke to the smaller ones, such as Chad Valley, Burnett, Bowman, Jubb, Wells, Carson, Bonds, Mills, Brimtoy, Bar Knight, Leeds Model Company and many others. We are always taking in consignments for all our sales and are very happy to visit as we travel around the country picking up collections of trains, toys and toy figures.

For further information on the Trains Galore auction and our other regular sales, or to get a valuation, please contact Hugo Marsh or Bob Leggett on
+ (0)1635 580595 or hugo@specialauctionservices.com

81 Greenham Business Park, Newbury RG19 6HW   www.specialauctionservices.com